[Fig 1] **Engraving of Trent Park, mid-19th century**
Hodson and Ford, *History of Enfield, 1873*

Trent Park: A History

PATRICK CAMPBELL

Incorporating material from
Stephen Doree's *Trent Park: A Short History to 1939*

First published in 1997 by Middlesex University Press

Middlesex University Press is an imprint of
Middlesex University Services Limited,
Bounds Green Road, London N11 2NQ

Copyright   Patrick Campbell 1997

All rights reserved. No part of this publication may be reproduced, stored in any retrieval system or transmitted in any form or by any means, electronic, mechanical, photocopying, recording or otherwise, without prior written permission of the copyright holder for which application should be addressed in the first instance to the publishers. No liability shall be attached to the author, the copyright holder or the publishers for loss or damage of any nature suffered as a result of reliance on the reproduction of any of the contents of this publication or any errors or omissions in its contents.

A CIP catalogue record for this book is available from
The British Library

ISBN 1 898253 17 X

Manufacture coordinated in UK by
Book in Hand Ltd London N6 5AH

Cover: The Mansion, Trent Park as it is today

Foreword

Royalty, aristocracy, wildlife and wild times have all played their part in the making of modern Trent Park. Latterly, of course, academia has helped to shape the place. Since the Second World War, Trent Park has played host to a teacher training college and a leading polytechnic. It is now the premier campus for one of the largest universities in the country — and a major centre for dance and drama education.

But while Middlesex University is one of Trent Park's current custodians — together with the London Borough of Enfield — it is only one of numerous 'landlords' who have had the good fortune to reside in this nook of natural beauty in north London.

This sense of history is something I feel particularly strongly. For while Trent Park dates back to before the Doomsday Book, I have been Middlesex University Vice-Chancellor for less than twelve months. I took over from Professor David Melville, the university's first Vice-Chancellor, in October 1996.

Like all who have been in residence here, Middlesex University is determined to play its part in protecting the area for future generations. Though the campus takes up only a fraction of Trent Park's expanse, it is at the heart of the thousand-acre site and features many of its most prominent landmarks — not least the fine eighteenth-century style mansion.

Middlesex University extends the warmest of welcomes to everyone who would like to pass through the campus as part of their trip to Trent Park. We are house proud — who wouldn't be — but we encourage as many people as possible to share our fine views and fresh air.

Patrick Campbell's *Trent Park: A History*, is a book for anyone who would like to know more about the personalities who have been drawn here in the past. I can promise surprises, high jinks and the occasional whiff of scandal. I am also delighted to report that much of the natural splendour of the place remains as it was when Henry IV cherished Trent Park for its open woodland and wildlife. Our own conservation plans include preservation of the campus grounds and landscaped features like the arboretum.

I wish you pleasant reading — and hope you will continue to enjoy Trent Park for many years to come.

Michael Driscoll, July 1997

Acknowledgments

I would like to thank a number of people who have contributed in varied ways to the making of this book. By far my greatest debt, inevitably, is to Stephen Doree whose *Trent Park: A Short History* expertly adumbrates the progress of the estate from hunting park to stately home. The fruits of his research are everywhere in evidence in the opening two sections of this account which remain very much as he wrote them. Douglas Dawson of the Conservation Committee has been consistently encouraging and has offered pertinent information about the estate as has Neil Billam of Enfield Leisure Services. The anecdotal material provided by Alec and Louvaine Dale has been particularly valuable: as head gardener during the Sassoon era and beyond, Alec is in a unique position to 'read between the lines' of recent commentary about Trent Park. Clive Fleay of the School of History has generously supplied many of the Country Life photographs which appear in the text. My thanks are due respectively to Camilla Costello of *Country Life* and to Dermot Chichester and Francois Rothlisburger of Christies, Manson and Wood Ltd for permission to use the splendid 1931 illustrations of Trent Park and the 'objets d'art' from the house auctioned at the Houghton sale and reproduced in Christies' catalogue of 8 December 1994. Finally I would like to tender my thanks to John Freeman who scrupulously edited much of the typescript and to past and present incumbents of the first floor of the mansion – David Melville and Ken Goulding – who have encouraged the project at various stages since its inception. The publication's appearance – in both senses of the word – is a measure of the enthusiasm and assiduity of Bobby de Joia, of Ann Lea who patiently word-processed my often illegible manuscript, of Teresa Kelly who prepared the typescript for the final stages and of Susan Scott and Marion Locke who saw it through to completion.

Patrick Campbell
Middlesex University

Contents

I
Enfield Chace to Trent Place
page 1

II
Trent: Loggia to Mansion
page 9

III
Trent Palladian
page 23

IV
Trent: A Prisoner of War
page 41

V
Trent Park Renascent
page 44

VI
Trent: Campus and Country Park
page 51

VII
Notes
page 61

VIII
List of illustrations
page 65

[Fig 2] Trent Place, 1808
Engraving by Sturt, 1808

I
Enfield Chase to Trent Place[1]

In the year 1676, the diarist John Evelyn rode out from Enfield to West Lodge, then the home of Henry Coventry, a minister of Charles II. As he travelled along Camlet Way (now the Hadley Road) he was amazed:

> That which I wondered at was that, in the compass of 24 miles, yet within 14 (miles) from London, there is not a house, barn, church or building besides three great lodges. To this lodge (West Lodge) are three great ponds and some few enclosures, the rest a solitary desert yet stored with not less than 3000 deer. These are pretty retreats for gentlemen, especially those who are studious and lovers of privacy[2].

Evelyn was describing Enfield Chase, then a vast hunting-ground, its perimeter marked by the settlements at Enfield, Cheshunt, Northaw, South Mimms, Barnet and Edmonton (Hadley being within the Chase). Of that vast area there survives today under 1000 acres to remind us what the Chase was once like: Trent Park. What gives Trent Park its distinctive character is that it has survived almost unchanged from those days when it served as open hunting-ground. The name 'Trent' – relatively recent – dates from the last 20 years of the 18th century, but the scenery of Trent Park is immensely ancient, a relic of a great hunting-park which was already old when Evelyn wrote, already venerable when the Norman-French word 'Chase' was first used to describe it in the 14th century, and probably well established when Domesday Book in 1086 stated 'there is a park there' when referring to Enfield[3]. Apart from some possible smallscale agriculture in the immediate vicinity of Camlet House (which was dismantled in 1440[4], its earlier history being, as yet, obscure) the great central area of Enfield Chase had never been under the plough. This was partly the result of the sheer poverty of the soil, but it was even more the result of a deliberate policy on the part of its owners and the public authorities over many centuries to isolate Enfield Chase from agricultural exploitation in the interests of preserving the game, the 'animals of the chase'.

To whom did the Chase belong? Oddly enough, there would have been various answers to this question at every point in its history. It is easy to identify the successive lords of the estate: the earliest known lord, Ansgar, one of the constables of Edward the Confessor, had inherited Enfield from his ancestors, and had in turn yielded it to Geoffrey de Mandeville after 1066[5]; from the Mandevilles it passed by marriage to the de Bohuns, from whom it passed by marriage, in the 14th century, to the usurper Henry Bolingbroke, Duke of Lancaster, who made himself king as Henry IV in 1399. From 1399, therefore, Enfield Chase, or Chace (as it was now called) was royal land, but administered separately from the bulk of Crown lands by the officials of the Duchy of Lancaster (which became a separate office in 1399 to administer the personal lands of the monarch, and which continues to this day). Much of the area of the former Enfield Chase is still held by the Duchy of Lancaster (as Trent Park was till 1923).

But if we seek to identify those who held rights in Enfield Chase, the question becomes much more complex. There were four broad types of right which might be widely dispersed. First, the right to hunt the deer was, in historic times, restricted to the lord and his nominees, and this embargo was enforced by a panoply of Chase courts; the lords of this Chase did not, apparently, claim the right of warren, that is, the exclusive right to hunt the rabbit, and it is possible that neighbouring villagers were permitted to hunt the lesser creatures of the Chase. Nonetheless it is clear that, whether legally permitted or not, the local peasants did in fact pursue all the animals in search of a more varied diet, risking considerable penalties in doing so[6]. A second sort of right was that of wayfaring, namely, the right to pass over the Chase if one was making a journey to some specific destination. A late 16th century map shows the Chase criss-crossed with paths – much as its wooded areas are today – while one of the earliest maps[7] of the Chase, in 1658, shows, among others, a path running north from Bourne Gate past Camlet to Cattlegate which, according to Nathaniel Salmon writing in 1728[8], was part of a London-Yarmouth road network. A third right was that of pasturing pigs and cattle on the Chase. This was an ancient right, well established by the time of the Norman Conquest, and enjoyed by the tenants of the Mandeville, de Bohun and Lancastrian lords; to the peasants of the settlements in Enfield, Edmonton, Mimms and Hadley, the Chase was therefore a vast open common. The same groups enjoyed a fourth right, that of taking underwood from the Chase for the purposes of fuel and house construction[9]. Theoretically, such privileges extended to the central areas of the Chase, including those now covered by Trent Park; but in practice, so difficult were the communications across the Chase, how many peasants bothered to exercise their rights to collect wood so far from home must be a matter for speculation.

It was not kindness on the part of the lords which guaranteed these rights to the peasants, but rather immemorial tradition, and such 'rights of common', as they were called, were

[Fig 3]
The Bevan Family at Trent Park, c1888
N Webster, *Spacious Days*

[Fig 4]
The staff at Trent Park c1888
N Webster, *Spacious Days*

theoretically tolerated on condition the 'commoners' did not take advantage of their privileges by exposing their pasture to the ploughs. In practice, however, it proved difficult to prevent commoners from enclosing the odd acre and adding it to their tenements, or even from running up a shack and squatting on the Chase itself. Such was the scale of peasant encroachments on the Chase and the felling of timber that John Norden was apprehensive of the future when he visited it in 1594:

> *Enfield Chase, a common of great comfort to the inhabitants near it for pasture, pannage and wood and other necessaries. But of late years, (the) wood hath fast decayed, insomuch that it is to be feared that the Chase will hardly yield fuel for the inhabitants, as by custom beyond memory they have had*[10].

The indications are that by the 17th century, population pressures in the local communities had created a land-hungry peasantry which turned covetous eyes on the great common which was Enfield Chase.

Thus various ways of life – hunter, pastoralist and agriculturalist – competed for supremacy in the Chase. While hunting remained the principal sport of kings, Enfield Chase would continue to be a royal hunting-ground, even within diminished boundaries. The last monarchs to hunt deer in the Chase, however, were Elizabeth I and James I, the latter of whom hived off part of the area to form his new and very private hunting enclosure of Theobalds Park in northern Enfield and southern Cheshunt[11]. After 1625, though monarchs long retained an interest in hunting, few if any ever drew the woodlands of Enfield Chase. Whatever the reason for this switch in royal preferences, the eventual result could not be in doubt: as the royal commitment to hunting declined, so the pressures to turn the Chase into an area of farmland grew more intense.

Meanwhile, outside interests had begun to influence developments on the Chase. As London spread its tentacles in all directions, so John Norden had noticed as early as 1594 that 'the merchants of London take up the best seats in Middlesex... for their recreation in summer time and for withdrawing places in times of sickness'. As a consequence, the

[Fig 5]
**Trent Park,
North front, 1890**
N Webster,
Spacious Days

value of the Chase began to appreciate as real estate, quite apart from its value as potential farmland. But the bar to enrichment – for speculators and farmers alike – was the Crown itself, owner of the Chase and the ultimate authority behind the Chase courts.

That barrier was suddenly removed in the 1640s, when the power of the Crown was smashed in a successful Civil War. Within months of the execution of Charles I in 1649, the first disturbances were reported from the Chase, as commoners scrambled to hunt the deer and fell the valuable timber in defiance of the Chase courts, which appealed to the new public authorities for assistance and direction[12]. But whatever interests the new republican government of 1649 represented, it did not represent the interests of the peasantry. The Commonwealth judged that Enfield Chase was too valuable a prize to allow its resources to be wantonly destroyed by the local inhabitants, especially in view of Parliament's need to find new funds to pay off its own troops and send them home. Though the motivation might be different, the republican government therefore decided to resist peasant encroachments and depredations even more vigorously than had the officials of the Crown. In 1654, the Cromwellian Council of State ordered that the Chase should be surveyed, divided into a smaller number of allotments, and then sold to the highest bidders for ready cash; only a small area was set aside to look after local rights of common[13].

[Fig 6]
Trent Park south front, 1890
N Webster,
Spacious Days

The survey was duly made in 1656, the first allotments were sold off, and substantial newcomers began to enclose farms and build houses on the Chase. But inadequate provision had been made for the local commoners, and the result was a minor 'civil war' which flared up on the Chase in 1659 when a 'rude multitude' from Enfield broke into the new farms, pulled up the hedges, filled in the ditches and smashed up the houses. The government ordered in two troops of cavalry to deal with the opponents of its orders[14]. But no general civil war followed on the Chase. Within nine months the Republican government had come to an end and Charles II was 'restored' to the throne. Enfield Chase was restored along with the monarchy, Cromwell's divisions of the Chase were scrapped, and those who had bought allotments surrendered them back to the Crown. But it soon became apparent what had been at the bottom of the riots on the Chase: in an appeal to Parliament in November 1660, the inhabitants of Enfield alleged that between 200 and 300 poor families had moved to Enfield and settled on or near the Chase during the previous decade or so[15]. In the Enfield area alone perhaps a thousand settlers had colonised the Chase during those disturbed years. Since an armed republican government had been unable to remove them, the restored monarchical government, with only a tiny standing army, must perforce allow them to remain. Enfield Chase was thus given a new lease of life. Its extent was now less than before the Civil War, but the great central area survived as the 'solitary desert' visited by John Evelyn in 1676.

Evelyn saw the deer and the woodlands: he did not see the poachers and the despoilers of the timber. As the Chase continued to shrink (in 1700 it was estimated to be only half the size it had once been), so the local inhabitants were able to extend the range of their predatory operations into the very heart of the Chase. Sixty years later, the novelist Daniel Defoe picked up the story of what had happened[16]:

> *After the Restoration, it was reassumed and laid out again; woods and groves were everywhere planted, and the whole Chase restored with deer. But the young timber, which indeed*

began to thrive, was so continually plundered, and the deer-stealers so harassed the deer... that the place was almost ruined as a forest, and little but hares and brushwood was to be found in it.

Nonetheless Defoe was optimistic that the Chase could be restored as a royal hunting-ground:

But now we hear that, by the vigilance of General Pepper, the Chace is much recovered, and likely to be a place fit for the diversion of a prince as it had been before.

[Fig 7]
Sir Philip Sassoon by John Singer Sargent, 1923, The Tate Gallery

Unfortunately Defoe's optimism was misplaced. General Pepper and other rangers found the problem of dealing with the local inhabitants insurmountable. Pepper himself complained, in 1716, that poachers had reduced the number of deer from 'several thousands to a few hundred', and he recognised that, unless the local inhabitants could be restrained from using the Chase as one vast common, there was little chance of restoring the Chase to its former glories as a royal hunting-ground[17]. In the event, the days of the Chase as a place fit for the diversion of princes were over. But this did not mean that the Chase was simply surrendered into the hands of the local peasantry. With the increase in population that occurred in the 18th century, and the relentless growth of metropolitan London, the future of Enfield Chase came to be determined by groups other than royal hunters or peasant farmers. Two sorts of outsider cast covetous eyes on the Chase. The first were the successful London businessmen who, since Norden's day, had not ceased to look for country retreats and for opportunities of converting mercantile wealth into real estate: a 17th century proverb reckoned that 'he who buys an estate in Hertfordshire pays two years' purchase for the air of it'[18], and in terms of amenity, Hertfordshire began at Enfield Chase.

The second outside group were the agricultural improvers, who yearned to sweep away traditional open fields and commons and replace them with enclosed farms of cornlands. Notable among these was Arthur Young of North Mymms, who commented on Enfield Chase in 1770. Where Evelyn had seen beauty and an enviable privacy, Young saw only a system of organised torpor, a tiresome relic of the past:

So large a tract of waste land, so near the capital, within the reach of London as a market and as a dung-hill is a real nuisance to the public. The soil is capable of yielding any production... the luxuriant growth of the spontaneous productions prove sufficiently what the cultivated ones might

[Fig 8] The south front with its 1890s facade of mauve brick

be. If this tract of useless land was enclosed, with farm houses and proper offices built, it would let at once for 15 shillings an acre.

Consequently Young recommended George III to consider that 'the good of the whole nation is in proportion to the increase of the profit of the Crown'[19].

The powerful conjunction of these two groups of outside interests brought the Chase to an end. In 1777, after a decade of rumour and speculation, these interests succeeded in persuading the king, ever jealous of his reputation as 'farmer George', to consent to an Act of Parliament to dis-chase, divide and enclose Enfield Chase[20]. The Act began with an obeisance in the direction of improved agriculture:

> *And whereas the Chase, in its present state, yields very little profit, either to the King's Majesty, or to the said freeholders and copyholders, or their tenants, in comparison with what it might do if the same was divided and improved...*

Once passed, the Act lopped off large areas around the fringes of the Chase and assigned them to some of the neighbouring parishes, farms and tithe owners in lieu of extinguished rights of common. The remaining area, itself a mere fraction of the medieval Chase, was divided into 'lots'[21] which were then to be leased on terms which should promote agricultural improvement and augment the revenue of the Crown. Because the costs of converting virgin soil to farmland were expected to be high, all the lessees were required to be men of substance, though it was later a matter of regret to professional agricultural improvers that too many lots had fallen into the hands of retired London tradesmen with little or no experience of farming[22].

Enfield Chase was thus legislated out of existence. The improvers had won. But lingering sentiment also prevailed in the end. Among its many clauses, the Act provided that, 'when... any of His majesty's lands... be inclosed with pales and be converted into a park', the deer should enjoy the protection of the ancient park laws. The Act thus provided that a miniature hunting-park should be set up in the midst of the former Chase, and lots 21 and 22 were earmarked for this purpose. The man who obtained the lease of this principal Crown allotment had virtually no experience of either hunting or of agriculture, but he had powerful connections at court: he was the physician of the royal household, Dr Richard Jebb. Jebb was to create that miniature deer park, an Enfield Chase in microcosm (though the name followed later) – Trent Park.

[Fig 9]
The south front, 1931

II
Trent: Loggia to Mansion

Within 10 years of the passing of the 1777 Act, Trent Park's house and estate had begun to take shape.

The name 'Trent' echoed Jebb's own colourful career as a royal doctor. He was a strange man who served a strange master, George III. A man of strong opinions, tactless to the point of insanity, urging remedies as drastic as they were hazardous, Jebb rose in the esteem of sick London society until he was earning over £6,000 a year in fees[23] (at a time

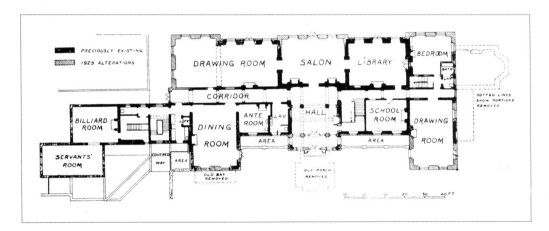

[Fig 10]
Ground floor plan of Trent Park, 1931

when a labourer was passing rich on £20). His reputation soared when he hurried out to Trento in the Austrian Tyrol early in 1777 in order to save the life of the king's younger brother, the Duke of Gloucester, who was suffering from a malady that modern physicians would probably diagnose as psychosomatic. The duke recovered under the impact of the doctor's ranting hit-and-miss methods, and the royal Lazarus was restored to the king's tearful embrace in October 1777[24]; two months later, Dr Jebb secured the lease of lots 21 and 22 (together with lot 20, an agricultural lot) in the former Enfield Chase, as a favoured tenant of the king. Six months later he was created a baronet, and took the title Sir Richard Jebb of Trent Place. Rumour had it that George III insisted on the name of 'Trent'.

The lease laid on Jebb the obligation to 'lay out the sum of £385 at the least in and about erecting substantial and convenient buildings', to construct a fence around the deer park and to lay drains. The rent of all three lots, totalling 385 acres, was £148 a year[25].

Jebb quickly set about building a house on Noddingswell Hill above the meeting point of three streams known in 1777 as the 'Three Partings'. A sketch by Willey Reveley in the early 1780s shows 'a lodge on Enfield Chase altered by Sir W Chambers for Sir R Jebb'[26]; a sale catalogue of 1787 mentions that 'the principal front is decorated with

[Fig 11]
Zoffany: The Colmore Family: over the Drawing Room chimney piece, 1931

noble columns, and pilasters, dental cornice, ballustrades, flights of stone steps etc'[27]. Reveley's sketch depicts a villa on two floors, surmounted by a small dome, and with a central door flanked by a pair of upper and lower windows. That this house was not the first built by Jebb on this site is confirmed by the Gentleman's Magazine for 1787:

> *It appears that the Enfield Chase villa, ill-contrived as it is,*
> *and more than once altered, consumed above £19,000.*

The same author, who evidently disapproved of Jebb's taste, went on to describe his villa in faintly mocking terms[28]:

> *The loggia, for such it should rather be called than a house, being hardly calculated for a single man and his servants, is only about thirty feet by forty, and the largest room scarce twenty feet by sixteen, the best bed chamber seventeen by twelve and nine feet high, and the kitchen fifteen by eleven.*

Trent helped to bankrupt Richard Jebb. Though a rich man, he died in debt, and he instructed his executors to sell the house. Such was the penalty of establishing a gentleman's residence and farm on virgin soil, in the midst of a former royal hunting-ground.

Jebb's house is still there. Enter the present mansion by the main (south) entrance, and there before you is the lower half of the facade of the villa that Chambers altered for Jebb, exactly as Reveley depicted it 190 years ago, save that there are now recesses in the walls instead of windows.

In addition to the house, farm buildings had already appeared:

> *The offices form a large quadrangle, at a proper distance from the house, including every accommodation for farming, besides bed-chambers, library, billiard room, and other distinct conveniences. At the back of this there is an excellent kitchen garden of three acres, walled and planted with fruit trees in a most prolific state, with a grand walk, eight hundred feet long and eleven feet wide, and a paved melon ground. The approach to the premises is by iron gates and a double lodge.*

[Fig 12]
Looking west:
The Drawing Room,
1931

[Fig 13]
Looking east: The
Drawing Room, 1931

Where Jebb built that structure there stands today the stable block: the buildings themselves may possibly date from the mid-19th century, but successive editions of the Ordnance Survey maps reveal that not merely the site but also the basic quadrangular plan of the stable block date from the early 19th century, and almost certainly from the 1780s. Moreover, the kitchen garden still survives at the 'back' of this building and is still partially enclosed by its brick wall 'twelve feet high and firmly secured by buttresses', exactly as the sale catalogue of 1787 described it.

There had also been a certain amount of landscaping of the grounds by 1787: 'At the back of the house is a piece of water, formed after the buildings were completed'[29]. This confirms that the Jebb house faced south, away from the lake, and that the earliest landscaping had taken place sometime between 1783 and 1787. Once again, the sale catalogue provides a verbal description:

> *Near this approach, Nature has furnished a supply of water, which Art has rendered of pleasing form and beautiful effect, much heightened by a noble oak, apparently springing from its bed, encircling which and bordering the water are neat gravel walks; shrubberies and plantations on either side adorn the boundaries of the estate.*

A persistent 20th century tradition associates Sir Humphrey Repton with this first landscaping[30], but there seems to be no documentary evidence either to support or to deny this claim. On the other hand, there is evidence associating the royal architect, Sir William Chambers, with the house itself, and it is not beyond the bounds of possibility that either he or a pupil may have had a hand in landscaping the park.

To sum up Jebb's achievement: in the ten years in which he was the proprietor, he established the name of 'Trent', created a deer park, built a small villa, constructed the 'offices', established a farm, and commissioned an artist to form a lake at the point where the 'Three Partings' met. It is surprising how much of Jebb's legacy can still be recognised today.

[Fig 14]
Lacquer and Delftware in the Drawing Room, 1931

Sometime during the twenty years following Jebb's death in 1787, the house was enlarged by the addition of a wing at each end, thus doubling its length. The author of this enlargement was either the Earl of Cholmondeley, who bought the estate in 1787, or John Wigston of Edmonton, to whom Lord Cholmondeley sold it in 1793. Wigston held the lease from 1793 to 1810[31] and is known to have spent lavishly, not only on the house, but also on the estate, where he tried with little success to raise a crop of wheat from the poor gravelly soil (incidentally informing Arthur Young of his expensive failure)[32]. The earliest visual evidence of this enlarged house is an engraving of 1808, which depicts the villa from the north side, standing on rising ground above the lake[32a]. The outline of this house, with its gently curving three central bays, can be traced in all subsequent pictures of the north side until 1923, and an alignment of the photographic evidence of 1923 and 1930[33] clearly shows that nine of the windows of the present staff common room correspond exactly to the nine windows of the 1808 house [Figs 5, p4; 6, p5].

A sale notice of August 1807 in *The Times* helps to corroborate the identification[34]:

> *Elegant modern residence, comprising a suite of three principal saloons, superbly decorated at great expense, besides every accommodation for a family of the first fashion.*

These three 'saloons' have survived all subsequent changes, and correspond to the three principal divisions of the present staff common room, wedged as it still is between the facade of the early 1800s and Jebb's facade of the early 1780s.

[Fig 15] Enfilade from Library, through Saloon, to Drawing Room, 1931

[Fig 16]
New overmantel panel in the Blue Room: printed in red and blue by Mr Rex Whistler, 1931

In 1810 Trent Park was sold to Sir Henry Lushington, who went bankrupt and who sold it to John Cumming, a London merchant, in 1813[35]. An engraving of 1815 shows the house exactly as it had been in 1808, but the author of *The Beauties of Middlesex* in 1816 saw interesting changes afoot[36]:

> The mansion... is a spacious brick structure, lately whitened, and is on a fine swell of land in the midst of an attached park. The whole of the grounds, enclosed within park pales, comprises very nearly five hundred acres... A valley immediately in front of the dwelling is ornamented with a fine sheet of water. Very considerable improvements in the house and grounds at this time in a state of progress under the direction of the present proprietor, John Cumming Esq.

[Fig 17a] The Blue Room, pale grey walls, red lacquer

The author did not explain what these 'improvements' were; nor did 'Ambulator', who in 1825 reported that 'Cumming has lately made many improvements'[37]. The only indication is provided by another sale notice, this time of December 1832 shortly after Cumming died[38]: having made the point that Cumming had spent the princely sum of £35,000 on bringing Trent Park 'to its present state of perfection', the notice goes on to refer to five principal rooms – library, chamber, saloon, dining-room and gentleman's room; there was also a hall, attic, basement, housekeeper's room and kitchen. Clearly, Cumming had added two principal rooms, a dining-room and a gentlemen's room, as well as a hall and an attic. The mention of the hall implies that he must have extended the house on the south side thereby screening Jebb's original south facade from view. Moreover, since the present mansion has retained from its predecessor five principal rooms and a hall, there are very good grounds for believing that the basic pattern of the ground floor of the mansion, as it is now, had taken shape before 1832, probably before 1830 when Cumming successfully applied to the Duchy of Lancaster for an early renewal of the 99-year lease, to run from 1831 to 1930[39]. This basic pattern certainly existed in 1866 when the first 25-inch Ordnance Survey map of the area was published.

Cumming's legacy was an impressive one. Nonetheless the sale notice possibly exaggerated in describing the park as 'a magnificent domain' and the house as a 'noble mansion' containing a suite of splendid apartments with every other necessary appendage to the accommodation of a nobleman's establishment or family of the first consequence.

The leasehold property was not bought by a nobleman, however, but by a banker of recent Quaker antecedents, David Bevan who, according to a family tradition, bought Trent Park while asleep at the auction![40] Four years later, in 1837, he transferred the property to his eldest son, Robert Cooper Lee Bevan, who was to reside at Trent for the next 53 years at the head of a Victorian family. Thus Trent Park became a family home, perhaps for the first time. The surviving evidence about Trent Park during Robert Bevan's long proprietorship is, however, disappointingly meagre. The most substantial description occurs in the second edition of *The Beauties of Middlesex* published in 1850[41]:

> *This estate is entered from the high road, about mid-way between Southgate and Potters Bar, by a pair of handsome gates, with wicket gates connected with the lodges at each side. The approach sweeps in with a fine bold approach to the left, then enters a grove, through which it passes to an avenue of young lime trees, about a quarter of a mile long, then enters a wood... and winds down through a lawn to the front of the house. This avenue is planted with two rows at either side to form, at some time, a centre arch with two aisles. This avenue will be beautiful at some future day, but will require a large mansion at the head of it to give magnificence and a noble background to the approach... The house is a spacious brick building, stuccoed, and is seated on a fine swell of land in the midst of a park of 700 acres. The whole is enclosed within park pales... To the north front is a beautiful lawn, sloping down to the waters of the lake.*

To this writer, therefore, the house of 1850 was 'spacious', but did not constitute 'a large mansion'. If our central hypothesis is valid, he was describing the house more or less as John Cumming had left it.

Unfortunately, there is no corresponding visual evidence for a further 23 years, until 1873 when a miniature print[42] shows the north side of the house for the first time since 1815. As expected, there had been extensions to the west and east of the earlier house, and a room had been built above the original Jebb loggia. Thus far, these extensions could represent the Cumming house of 1832. But what cannot be reconciled with the details of the Cumming house is a tower which had appeared on the east side of the house. This tower and its appurtenances must therefore have been created by one of the Bevans, probably Robert. However, a photograph of 1890[43] shows this side of the house exactly as it had been in 1873 and conclusively proves that Robert Bevan was not an active builder on this side of his house for the last 20 years or so of his life.

[Fig 17b]
The Blue Room, Trent Park by Winston Churchill. Exhibition Royal Academy, 1948

- 17 -

[Fig 19a]
The Library: deep yellow walls, 1931

A photograph of the same year, 1890[44], simultaneously reveals the appearance of the south side of the house for the first time since Reveley's sketch of the early 1780s. And what a difference! From this picture, the house appears as a stuccoed mansion built irregularly on two or three floors, the elegant string-course barely concealing the fact that compartment had been added to compartment over a period of time. If the hypothesis concerning Cumming's improvement is valid, then much of the south facade as shown in this photograph of 1890 must represent the house as it had been in 1832. But, since there are many more rooms than can possibly be accounted for in the 1832 sale catalogue, it must equally follow that one or both Bevans had continued to add extensions and additions. This may possibly be corroborated by the three 'ghost' windows that can still be seen inside the mansion on the second floor towards the east: if these windows represent the location of the attic of 1832, then it would follow that the attics built to the south of this (the windows of which may just be described in the 1890 photograph) must represent the work of a Bevan. The reader must be warned, however, that this interpretation of the building history of the mansion is very speculative because the available evidence is fragmentary and unsatisfactory.

By the time these photographs were taken, Robert Bevan had died[45], and the estate had passed to his eldest son, Francis, the only time that Trent Park had passed from father to son by legacy. Francis planned a more up-to-date mansion, and successfully applied to the Duchy of Lancaster in 1893 for a £10,000 building grant, and the work of reconstruction must have begun soon afterwards[46].

The results can be seen in photographs of 1903[47]. On the south side, Francis Bevan replaced the jumble of rooms with an imposing facade built uniformly on three floors, with three projecting bays of unequal size. This asymetrical south facade was merely tidied up by Philip Sassoon in the 1920s, and is substantially the same structure today as it was in 1903. The east side of the house appears to have been little rebuilt, however, as *Country Life's* photograph of 1903 shows an ungainly accumulation of rooms, though the tower seems to have been tidied up. The north side of the house appears not to have been touched; it was still on the two floors that it had been 40 years earlier (one small third floor attic apart – the attic of 1832?).

[Fig 19b]
The Library: Looking West, 1931

Thus Francis Bevan's 're-building' of Trent was only partially completed. The new south front was given its modern appearance, but the east and north sides were largely left alone. Inside the house, there is a suggestion that he may have raised the floor levels, since the service wing at the west end of the house which survives to this day has landings which do not match the floor levels of the mansion: this can only mean that the first and second floors of the mansion have been raised since the service wing was built, whenever that was. When this problem is conclusively solved, it will cast further light on the building history of the mansion.

There was one final visible change in the 1890s: the colour of the mansion. Photographs of 1903 show that at long last the stucco had been removed, and a writer of 1903 confirmed this when he described the house as 'a large, red-brick pile, creeper-clad and bowered in woodland'[48]. But a different impression is conveyed by Osbert Sitwell, who had less enchanting memories of the house he had seen when a schoolboy, where 'glowered a mid-Victorian mansion of mauve brick, with designs in black brick covering its face, with a roof of mauve slate, turreted and slightly frenchified'[49].

Of 19th century Trent quite a lot survives. The disposition of the principal rooms is the same as in the early or mid-19th century, the south (main) front of the mansion is basically as it was constructed in the 1890s, and under its red-rose brick of the 1920s still presumably 'glowers' the 'mauve' brick seen by Sitwell and which can be seen to this day in the former service wing. The long rose gardens have gone, but the gardens on the east side, with their 'pink pillars'[50] may still be seen. The stable block, farm buildings and

[Fig 21]
The Saloon: buff and quiet green, 1931

cottages, where they have not survived unchanged from the 18th century, are of 19th century origin[51]. Even the landscape owes more to the 19th century than may at first sight appear: the limes along the Cockfosters Drive were planted by Robert Bevan in the 1840s, and many of the oaks of the estate owe their origin to Cumming's renewed lease

[Fig 22]
The Saloon with matching pair of George II side tables, 1931

of 1831 which committed him to a tree-planting policy that should ensure that there would be 10,000 oak trees by 1841 and 20,000 by 1856. Hence much of the sylvan landscape which so delights the eye was the outcome of deliberate 19th century policy.

[Fig 24] Dining Room (now the Green Room) showing Chinese screen, Zoffany conversation piece of young family and Whistler monogram (undermantle), 1931

III
Trent Palladian

Five years after completing his rebuilding programme, Francis Bevan sold the estate. The buyer was Sir Edward Sassoon, the extravagantly rich Jewish scion of an oriental merchant bank, baronet, MP for Hythe and friend of Edward VII[52].

A word about this family's un-English origins is in order. Members of the Sephardic sect, the Sassoons (the name 'Sason' means 'joy' in Hebrew), who claimed descent from King David, had flourished in Baghdad for centuries, trading in – among other things, opium. During the eighteenth century their power and influence declined and the family were forced to flee, first to Bushire in Persia and then to Bombay, a fast-growing port and the natural entrepot for a trade with East Africa and the Gulf that involved bartering a range of goods – silk, spices and pearls – for Indian cotton. To encourage business, the Sassoons created financial trading facilities, including a counting house and wharfages which allowed them to deal directly with the fleets of dhows bringing these exotic commodities across the Indian Ocean. Ever alert to commercial possibilities and benefiting from the protection afforded by British rule in India, David Sassoon subsequently expanded into China: his company was thus adroitly placed to exploit the growing trade between England (by now the principal exporter of finished cotton goods) and China. As Stanley Jackson's *The Sassoons* makes clear, 'the frenzied demand for India's cotton transformed her economy and catapulted the Sassoons into an

[Fig 25]
A side table in the Dining Room, 1931

[Fig 26]
The corridor crossing the Entrance Hall. Staircase just in view, 1931

unprecedented prosperity and influence'[53]. By the turn of the century much of the business of David Sassoon and Sons was being conducted from London and the family, long loyal to Britain and the imperialist ethic, was being assimilated into British high society. As grandson of David Sassoon, Sir Edward Sassoon's decision to purchase Trent Park was part of this process; its acquisition would enable him to play the part of a country gentleman at a relaxed weekend retreat, away from the intense social atmosphere that characterised life at 25 Park Lane, his town residence. But before he had much time to develop the Trent Park estate or even to enjoy its existing parks and woodland, he died of cancer. He was only fifty-six, the year 1912.

Trent Park now became the property of his son. Eldest son of an eldest son, it fell to Philip Albert Gustave David, the third baronet, of Kensington Gore and Eastern Terrace, Brighton, to continue, along with his sister Sybil, the brilliant social tradition of the Edwardian Sassoons [Fig 7, p6]. He was well suited to the task. At the age of 24, Sir Philip was already, despite his Jewish origins, promising to be more English than the English – or at least more refined. There was no doubt that he was already richer than most of his associates. As Roth says in his history of the Sassoon dynasty, he was 'born with the silver spoon in his mouth overlaid with gold, tipped with iridium and studded with oriental pearls'[54].

At Eton he cultivated the image of sybarite and dandy. Slim, reserved and 'exotic' looking, he unfortunately had a pronounced lisp to go with his guttural accent, a potential shortcoming suitably cushioned by his manifest wealth and connections. As a history student at Christ Church Oxford, he first acquired the reputation for entertaining on a lavishly ostentatious scale, on one occasion having 'a seven course banquet specially prepared by a London restaurant for a party in his rooms. It was kept hot on the train and served promptly at seven by a relay of college scouts'[55]. Like his soon to be celebrated cousin, the poet Siegfried, he rode with fashionable hunts such as the Heythrop, though he appeared more concerned to cut a dash with his Savile Row hunting pink than to develop a reputation as a horseman. Siegfried would not have approved. Neither apparently did all his Oxford cronies. There is a story of his being chased round Tom Quad by a fellow ex-Etonian with an Australian stock whip.

That story may be part of Sassoon folklore but the sudden accession to the family millions was an irrefutable fact – and one duly recorded by high society. Already rich from maternal bequests – his mother had died while he was an undergraduate – Philip

[Fig 27]
The Wistaria Walk (Pergola), 1990

was, at the age of twenty-three, in possession of most of his father's fortune – he inherited nearly a million pounds from his parents – his shares in the family company, a large collection of works of art from his Rothschild grandparents and – most important of all from this chronicler's perspective – the Sassoon properties, including Trent Park. In his will Sir Edward Sassoon had entertained the fond hope that his son would consolidate the company concerns 'so that its reputation and standing so laboriously built up by his ancestors for close on a century would not be tarnished or impaired by the possible neglect or mismanagement of outsiders'[56].

The paternal wish was not fulfilled. Sassoon's ambitions were social and political; his bent was for the glitter of the house party, not the graft of commerce. To this end he was duly adopted and voted in as Member of Parliament for his father's old seat at Hythe. Elected by a substantial majority of 1,700, he continued to represent the constituency until his death a quarter of a century later. But he declined, as a matter of principle, the salary due him as a politician and became known more for his studied elegance than his powers as a parliamentary orator.

In 1915, after a brief spell as aide de camp to Lord French, he became secretary to Field Marshal Haig. Both Sassoon and Haig had been members of the Bullingdon at Oxford, fellow devotees of polo. Now that the sterner business of war beckoned, Philip proved his value to Haig as a fluent communicator with the military chiefs in France, and as a political manipulator back home who could use his considerable social connections to lobby politicians, some of whom were beginning to question Haig's battle strategies and his propensity for 'speeding young heroes up the line to death'[57]. When Siegfried Sassoon mischievously sent *The Old Huntsman And Other Poems* (1917), to 'The Commander-in-Chief of the British Expeditionary Force', he did so in the certain knowledge that his

[Fig 28]
Daffodils in front of the mansion, 1982

second cousin would read his powerfully pacifist poems. But there was no conscientious objector lurking in Philip's soul...

[Fig 29]
Lily Ponds, 1931

After demobilisation, Philip, now 31, was appointed as parliamentary private secretary to Lloyd George. Roth points out that 'a caricature of 1921 shows an intensely semitic Sir Philip Sassoon pulling the strings that work a puppet Lloyd George' and wondering:

> *Why legislators, when at Lympne,*
> *Make such an awful fuss of him!*[58]

To play the role of 'puppet-master' was an important responsibility. Lloyd George hated paperwork, relying on his gifts as a speaker, and if necessary as an improviser. Sassoon, on the other hand had a meticulous eye for detail and made sure, via his carefully orchestrated lunches and dinners in the House, that he kept the prime minister in touch with grass-root opinion. And if Lloyd George had little time for the minutiae of memoranda and statistics, Sir Philip was on hand to supply the necessary facts. Above all his role as host was invaluable. At Port Lympne, several key post-war conferences were stage-managed by Philip, not least a 1920 gathering when the question of reparation was considered by the allies.

At one point it was rumoured, so well did Sir Philip hit it off with Lloyd George, that he might marry his daughter Megan. But the richest bachelor in England showed no inclination to take a wife or even a mistress. On the subject of matrimony he deflected questions with a stock rejoinder: 'I shall only marry when I find someone as lovely and perfect as my sister'[59]. He never did.

With his growing reputation as a socialite, allied to his 'exotic' background and apparent lack of red-bloodedness, Sir Philip himself now became a regular target for satire and caricature. The most celebrated lampoon began:

> *Sir Philip Sassoon is the member for Hythe:*
> *He is opulent, swarthy and jejune and lithe*

and concluded:

> *And the daughters of Britain will wish they were dead*
> *Once Sir Philip Sassoon has decided to wed*[60].

At his house parties 'the daughters of Britain' were usually safely married. But though Sir Philip might be a reluctant bridegroom, he was building on his already considerable reputation as a host, aware of the potential benefits to his burgeoning political career. The point was not lost on cousin Siegfried, who on hearing that Philip was giving a 'Hospital Ship' to the Ulster Rebellion, complained in a letter to Max Beerbohm that it was an 'awful example of buying political advancement'[61].

[Fig 30]
The flower borders, June 1930

If Port Lympne in Kent was ideally placed for European visitors and 25 Park Lane resplendent with Georgian silver, 18th Century French furniture, Aubusson carpets, chinoiserie, and Old Masters[62], was already renowned for its formal dinners and receptions, then Trent Park would be perfect, suitably refashioned and refurbished, for a very English activity: the glamorous country weekend. Philip set about gilding the lily with gusto. Trent Park had to be *made* beautiful, a country house in a style quintessentially English that reflected his own well-defined tastes. That Sir Philip fulfilled this ambition was in no small measure due to two strokes of good luck. First, he managed to secure the freehold of the estate, a 1923 acquisition which gave him 'carte-blanche' to re-build the mansion on a more palatial scale. Second, the demolition of Devonshire House, Piccadilly, the last of William Kent's London palaces, provided Sassoon with the other excuse he needed, the chance to acquire vast quantities of genuine 18th century bricks and other building materials such as stone string courses which he could re-use at Trent. The demolition of this 'low-built mansion, once so great' did not escape the notice of cousin Siegfried, whose 'Monody on the Demolition of Devonshire House' made reference to an historic and literary past now without a home:

> *Ducal, demure, secure in its estate –*
> *Where Byron rang the bell and limped upstairs*
> *And Lord knows what political affairs*
> *Got muddled and remodelled while Their Graces*
> *Manned unperturbed Elizabethan faces –*

If Siegfried felt elegiac about a 'Devonshire (God rest it) House' now unable to 'screen a mouse'[63], Philip saw its demise as a positive and material opportunity and plunged into the work of remodelling his own pile.

In accordance with the 18th century models he and his advisers worked from, Sassoon sought to make his mansion as symmetrical as possible: he was willing to demolish large areas and eradicate its unprepossessing Victorian features, but he was not prepared to destroy the old Bevan house completely [Fig 8; p7]; and, in any case, did not want the house out of commission too long as an entertainment centre, though he compromised by retaining the asymmetrical south wall more or less as Francis Bevan had left it in 1903, merely ripping down the creeper and pulling the porch and window bays back into line. On the east side he was prepared to be more drastic, and cut away a whole section, replacing it with a single 'classical' wall (complete with blank windows). The north front – the side that looks out over the terrace to the lake – was dramatically changed. First, a new floor was added to bring this side into line with the rest of the house. Second a broad terrace was constructed. Finally, Sassoon removed all the old windows, including those which dated from 1808, and replaced them with a regular series of windows of classical proportions, regardless of the internal floor levels. The 'flanking and central projections of the south front were made to correspond' (what were to become the Blue and Green Rooms abutted a great square of cobbles and paving')[64]. The west side received less attention: the servants' wing, clad in its original brick, was not re-modelled but left

[Fig 31]
Swimming pool and orangery, looking east, 1931

[Fig 32a]
The Emma Crewe
'Pineapple' acquired
by Sir Philip Sassoon
from Wrest Park in
1934

discreetly shrouded by bushes; in its turn, this wing served to conceal from view the mechanics of the optical illusion which suggests that Trent is a completely symmetrical house. The whole edifice (the servants' wing excepted) was then faced with William Kent's 18th century bricks – and lo!, the Victorian mauve mansion was transformed into a Palladian country house with a rose-red exterior [Fig 9, p8]. The entire external transmutation met with the discerning approval of *Country Life's* architectural correspondent. Reviewing the recently completed alterations for this most prestigious of publications in 1931, Christopher Hussey complimented the owner's 'tact' in creating an English country house from an 'amorphous Victorian building':

> *Only the simplest elements of architecture were used, but the materials and the form were handled with such understanding that the exterior can be regarded as typical of the traditional English house unaffected by foreign example or architectural vogue. Trent fits into the setting so perfectly and accords so well with our expectations of a great country house because its designer aimed at representing the spirit of English domestic architecture, instead of inventing a specific style. The result is a building at once traditional and modern, traditional in its materials and genial proportions, modern in its concentration on essentials alone and in its expression of purpose*[65].

Inside the house, now entered through an impressive pillared doorway that had graced Chesterfield House, Sassoon retained to a very large extent existing walls and partitions. He realised that the central east-west corridor around which the early 19th century house had expanded suited his purpose admirably. The removal of the projecting porch and its replacement by a wide inner hall gave a new prominence to this feature, now changed by the addition of classical mouldings and arches, that, seen from either end offered 'a most satisfying vista of light but solid forms'[66]. On the ground floor, he made skilful use of the three original rooms of 1780-1808 – the library, saloon and drawing room – by opening them up to form an intercommunicating suite of reception rooms that ran parallel to the central corridor. The front of the house was dominated by the two apartments which had been added, it is thought, by John Cumming: the dining room, though retaining this purpose, was re-named the 'Green Room', while the original 'gentleman's room' at the south-east end of the building was retained as a second drawing room and re-named the 'Blue Room'. In all this refurbishment, symmetry and balance were overriding concerns – just as they had been with the outside alterations. In resisting the temptation – indulged at Port Lympne – to experiment in 'various engaging styles within a more or less traditional shell,' Sassoon had, according to the overwrought language of *Country Life*, circumvented the 'more complex problems presented by the interior and chosen a safe path 'between the Scylla of period reproduction and the Charybdis of modernism, either of which would constitute at Trent a lapse from the living tradition informing the exterior'[67]. Of course none of these apartments were family rooms – as old paintings show they had been in the Bevan days. The overriding purpose was to entertain guests in a tasteful setting by means of lavish service, sumptuous meals, scintillating conversation, luxurious accommodation and a comprehensive range of indoor and outdoor pursuits. Such were the ingredients of a weekend house party, which Philip Sassoon turned into a social institution between the wars, and which he cultivated with the flair of an original artist. This was the purpose for which Trent was completely redesigned between 1925 and 1931 [Fig 10, p9].

Decorations and furnishings were an integral part of this unified design, but whereas the decorations survive in large part, the furnishings are gone. Nonetheless the *Country Life* photographs of the central suite of rooms give some sense of the Sassoon taste in paintings, furniture and porcelain. Most of the pictures were so-called 'conversation pieces', many like that of the Colmore family over the mantelpiece in the drawing room by Zoffany [Fig 11, p10]. Indeed such was Sassoon's interest in this genre that he hosted an exhibition of these paintings in 1930. His passion for 'chinoiserie' was reflected in the lacquered cabinets that flanked the Venetian window, in porcelain jars and the Chinese wallpaper of the saloon (a copy of an original in the Victoria and Albert Museum). Tapestries hung from the warm parchment walls of the drawing room, walls that were surmounted by a full entablature. [Figs 12, p11; 13, p12; 14, p13]. By standing in the library (now the Boardroom) and looking straight through to the Venetian window at the far end, one can still take in the 'magnificent enfilade' that would greet Sassoon as he left his bedroom on a mid-summer morning [Fig 15, p14].

The emphasis throughout the house was on balanced contrast and antithesis: the severe surfaces of the architecture juxtaposed to the softness of the furnishings, tapestries and draperies; the hard angularity of the rich mouldings in contrast to the flowing lines of the porcelain, the 'chinoiserie', the luminous Venetian window and its flanking dolphins, the 'PS' monograms. Yet the sense of symmetry also prevailed – in the library's central bookshelf which, both in its shape and converging Whistler figures, repeated the motif of the Venetian window at the other end of the airy interior [Figs 19a, p18; 19b, p19; 20, colour plate II]. The 'Blue Room', subsequently the subject of a painting by Sir Winston Churchill, [Fig 17b, p17] was the setting for a contrast between the red masculine principle and the blue feminine principle, but whereas the blue-grey walls remain, the red lacquer furniture sufficiently important to be featured in *Country Life*, has long since vanished along with the sprigged green chintz and blue and white pottery [Figs 17a, p16; 17b, p17; 18, colour plate I]. Only in the Rex Whistler panel of 1931, where Minerva, the goddess of the Arts of Peace, stares across at Mars the god of the Arts of War, is there an echo of Sassoon's original conception. Once again the principle of balance is made manifest in a mural which 'summarizes... the pale blue and scarlet that are the room's predominant colours'[68] [Fig 16, p15]. So too in the green dining room, occupying the south-west wing, we find a deliberate echo – with its subtly complementary coloration and matching Whistler motifs – of the blue drawing room's features [Figs 21, p20; 22, p21; 23, colour plate III; 24, p22; 25; p23].

In other respects Sassoon's mansion was socially conservative. The large ground floor reception rooms and the smaller ones on the first floor were planned with the entertainment and pleasure of guests in mind. Connecting these rooms and immediately to the east of the hall was a substantial half-turn staircase which survives to this day, an early Georgian oak structure with spiral balusters which had been imported from William Kent's mansion, and the only example in the mansion of antique woodwork. It is tempting to speculate that in its Piccadilly setting, it might formerly have felt the weight of Byron's club foot as he 'limped upstairs'[69] [Fig 26, p24]. True to form the footmen's quarters were in the basement where the housemaids had a sitting room. Other servants had bedrooms on the top floor (where the ceilings were noticeably lower) or at the rear of the house. The pantry in the basement boasted a dumb-waiter whereby hot dishes could be conveyed speedily upwards for the distinguished diners in the 'Green Room'[70].

Beyond the chintz furnishings of the drawing room and saloon, the grounds boasted a number of exotic features that reflected the tastes of their owner and his panache as a colourist. Tended by an army of gardeners, many of whom lived in the twenty or so cottages dotted around the estate, the area to the south-east of the great house was developed into a formal garden on a scale undreamed of by the Bevans. The sumptuous long borders which led to the existing pergola of Italian marble columns were the glory of the garden. Over-arched with oak cross timbers and clothed with 'vines, wistaria and clematis'[71] – the wistaria's venerable stems still hold the columns in a serpentine embrace – the pergola ended in a curved seat of white marble. [Fig 27, p25] To reach this point, one walked along a corridor of Lilium regale and on paving stones reputed to have come from Waterloo bridge[72]. Not a stone, one might say, was left unturned by Sir Philip in the creation of Trent Park. At the other end of the long borders the focus was provided by the 'rond point', near which was the lead statuary of Samson and the wrestlers. Beyond, a double line of limes led north-east to the lake and the water garden.

[Fig 32b] Renaissance statuary brought to Trent Park in the late 1920s

[Fig 32c]
Renaissance statuary on the lawn to the left of the mansion terrace (late 1920s)

From every coign of vantage, there was a profusion of bloom for the visitor to admire. A *Country Life* photograph of the herbaceous borders taken in June 1930 shows graduated banks of colour, delphiniums, hollyhocks, irises and lupins flanking the lawns and lily ponds and presided over by hedges of yew. A *Descriptive Guide to the Gardens*[71] offers more precise information to the visitor:

> *The borders consist of three pairs of long beds and are planted with a combination of herbaceous and annual flowers. They are organised for the months of June and July, so that every inch of space can be made to yield its contribution of colour... a progression of lemon and white, through the rich blues, pinks*

and purples of the middle, to the stronger and more fiery tones of scarlet and orange which lie beyond the oak. On each side of the borders lie four hedge-enclosed rose-gardens of simple design, each with a rectangular waterlily pool as a central feature, and framed by borders filled with groups of roses [Figs 29, p27; 30, p28]

Sir Robert Boothby remembered 'the blue bathing pool surrounded by such a profusion of lilies that the scent at night became almost overpowering'[73]. At the whim of Sir Philip and to astonish his guests, a new floral tapestry of bedding plants might miraculously appear overnight. In the other direction was the lake with its two bridges and water garden ablaze with azaleas in May or Himalayan lilies in July; to the left of the lake the eye was taken to the obelisk – a sword unsheathed from its scabbard – which guarded the outposts of the Sassoon empire. To the south of the mansion thousands of naturalised daffodils, planted by Sassoon in the late 1920s, provided a natural carpet of gold to greet the Easter guests as they sped along the drive and onto the paved forecourt [Fig 28, p26]. Every Spring they still reappear, a memorial to the vision of the man who planted them in such profusion.

In the eighteenth century walled garden, retained alongside the west side of the pergola and divided into a parterre of four squares by avenues of apple trees and flower beds, grew melons, peaches and apricots, nectarines and plums. In season these fruits would be sent, several times a week, at first by train and later on by aeroplane to Port Lympne. Every morning Alec Dale the head gardener would 'see to the flowers', providing cut blooms for the town house in Mayfair or, at weekends for the pleasure of Sir Philip's house guests. Though he only used Trent Park as a summer residence during May, June and July, Sassoon spared no expense. When the swimming pool was excavated to replace the sunken garden beyond the east wing, he not only installed heating (the tanks were hidden in the basement of the mansion under the Blue Room) but, as Alec Dale recalls, he erected temporary plywood silhouettes to achieve a 'trompe l'oeil' effect before the 'real' statues arrived[74]. Once in place the sphinxes were positioned on the balustrades and gilded in an attempt to harmonise, one assumes, with the golden chains which linked the Portland stone bollards of the forecourt and the monogrammed drainpipes of the mansion, which had also been treated with gold-leaf. So keen was the Sassoon eye for harmonious effects, that he gilded the horns of the park deer and even, on one occasion, had the Union Jack lowered from its flagpole on top of the mansion because it clashed with the sunset[75].

His sense of symmetry, equally fastidious, was not confined to the house. Sassoon had a penchant for the formal vista only partially satisfied by his obelisk perspective. Frustrated by a local council who refused his request for a continuous avenue of limes from the pineapple monument to the Cockfosters gate, he planted a column of trees to give the 'trompe l'oeil' effect of a straight road continuing beyond, the point marked by a second monolith where the Cockfosters drive veered left to meet the existing entrance[76]. If he could not re-site the gates, at least he could alter their character. In October 1928 he removed the wrought-iron ones and replaced them with heavy oak gates, flanked by the lions which had formally graced Devonshire House.

But by 1930 Trent Park was becoming more than a baronial pile with formal and floral vistas, an imposing rose-red brick facade and salons replete with exquisite Georgian and Queen Anne furnishings. A number of unexpected features greeted the first-time guest. On 'Repton's' main lake Sassoon introduced a number of very un-English birds – black Australian and black-necked as well as white swans, pink flamingoes, cranes, king penguins and pelicans. On the upper lake where the rushy cover was thicker, there were more than seventy varieties of water fowl including Harlequin, Longtail, Mandarin and Carolina ducks, Emperor, Maned, Red-breasted and Snow Geese. Special food arrived from London Zoo; the flamingoes were fed a diet of dried shrimps to heighten the roseate hues of their plumage. But while a man and his young assistant were assigned to care for these birds, Sassoon took especial delight in feeding the king penguins himself. If he were in residence he would personally give them their fish every morning and evening[77]. There was also the watery haven for the human guests, a swimming pool set between borders of lilies and flanked by tall beech hedges. At the far end, Sassoon's newly created orangery was reflected in its blue heated depths [Fig 31, p29]. A short stroll away was an imposingly large structure which housed an indoor tennis court.

There were other genuflections to modern living. On the other side of the lake, Sir Philip landscaped a nine-hole golf course some of whose gentle undulations are still just visible. Professionals and caddies were in daily attendance should the lord of the manor decide on a quick lesson or a whirlwind round. Apparently he played at a frenetic pace – 18 holes in 90 minutes – invariably accompanied by two caddies[78]. Driving from a first tee, now occupied by the Health Centre, he shanked and hooked with the best of them, including the Prime Minister and the Prince of Wales; there visiting Walker Cup teams from the United States came to practise as a way of acclimatising to English conditions. It is a curious irony that though barely a vestige remains of Sassoon's course today – even the pastureland of its former fairways was recently piled high with silt from the lake in accordance with EEC regulations – golf is still played, and by a much wider cross-section of the population, on Trent's parkland to the south.

If golf was one developing enthusiasm, flying was another, particularly after Sassoon's appointment as Under-Secretary to Sir Samuel Hoare, at the Air Ministry in 1924. Declaring 'I am enraptured with my job[79]', he held the post until 1929 and again from 1931 to 1937. One way of expressing his abiding belief in air power was to fly himself. The airfield which he built in the late 1920s was on ground now occupied by the fifteenth fairway of Trent Park Golf Club. Running parallel to the road which now links Snakes Lane and the Long Border Car Park – formerly Sassoon's tennis courts – it ended in a hangar which housed his various aircraft – by turns Avro, De Havilland, Moth, Dragonfly, Perceval. Guests were encouraged to enjoy these modern machines, each one decked out with the latest gadgets and painted in the old Etonian colours of black with a blue stripe. For Sassoon, now qualified as a pilot, it enabled him to make light work of the trip to Port Lympne or the West End. Not that opinions were unanimous about his skills as a pilot and about those of some of his friends. One member of Squadron 601, of which Sassoon was honorary Commander-in-Chief, dived over Trent Park and dropped his wireless aerial in the lake, killing some of the exotic birds in the process[80]. Sir Philip himself had one narrow squeak in his newest toy, a twin-engined Perceval. Forced down in a heavy cloudburst, he crash-landed and was trapped in his cockpit until help arrived.

None of this deterred 'the host with the most'. He might be lampooned or attacked in Parliament – 'his baroque is worse than his bite[81]' as one wag had it – but his socialite reputation was now at its climacteric. In the 1930s, with refurbishments now complete, it was estimated that Trent Park alone cost over £10,000 a year to maintain – incidentally the cost of the entire 1893 Bevan reconstruction – quite apart from any further alterations which Sassoon might decide upon. This hospitality required a battalion of cooks, butlers, servers and housemaids; they maintained standards of service that would have shamed the best hotel in the land.

Sassoon's attention to detail was as legendary as his generosity. Fresh flowers were provided (from the estate's gardens and greenhouses) in every guest room. Changed every day, they were chosen to match the curtains, and if necessary, dyed the right colour. Orchids were presented to the ladies before dinner; male guests found red carnations and cocktails awaiting them on their dressing tables. As Under-Secretary For Air – the appointment was entirely appropriate in view of Philip's enthusiasm for flying, civil aviation and aircraft design – he had no difficulty in luring the cream of fashionable society to his Trent Park weekends. It was the place to be. Winston Churchill was a regular guest, and at various times the charismatic presences of George Bernard Shaw, Charlie Chaplin, Lawrence of Arabia, and Thornton Wilder showed that Sir Philip did not neglect his role as patron of the arts. Apart from the frequent appearances of the Prince of Wales and other English royals, there were visits from the King and Queen of the Belgians. Anthony Eden would often drop in for a game of tennis or a swim in the heated pool. As war clouds loomed, Sassoon hosted a conference at Trent that sought to stem the rising tide of Fascism in Europe.

[Fig 32d]
Music block under construction, mansion in background
July 1971

[Fig 32e]
Music block under construction showing lily pond
July 1971

If Philip was a politician who failed to climb very high up the greasy pole of preferment – perhaps there was more innate resistance from the English establishment than he had envisaged – he was the friend of princes, baronets, ministers and celebrities, a modern Prince Charming in the inter-war years. With his finely drawn features – particularly prominent in the early Sargent portrait[82] [Fig 7, p6] – he certainly looked the part. Moreover he sounded it. Every syllable was precisely enunciated, his 'r's' rolled in the French manner. According to Cecil Beaton he invented the fashionable ripostes of 'I could-dern't care less' and 'I could-dern't agree with you more'. In all this socialising he was aided and abetted by his cousin, Hannah Gubbay. From 1931 onwards Hannah, who looked remarkably like Flora Sassoon, and whose husband was managing director of the Sassoon company, played the role of 'hostess with the mostest' with aplomb. Though she lived in Hertford Street, Mayfair, – a property now occupied by an exclusive gaming club – she began to spend an increasing amount of time with Philip. For it was now that Trent Park – literally – flowered, now that it assumed the role of great country house that Sassoon had wanted to bestow on it when he initiated his massive programme of development and expansion. Hannah Gubbay's role as hostess – since Sir Philip had declined to marry and his sister had long since become Lady Rocksavage – was crucial. For, Robert Boothby recalled, 'his hospitality was on an oriental scale'.

> *The summer weekend parties at Trent were unique, and in the highest degree enjoyable, but theatrical rather than intimate. He frankly loved success, and you could be sure of finding one or two of the reigning stars of the literary, film or sporting worlds, in addition to a fair sprinkling of politicians and – on occasion – royalty (the Sassoons never forgot that they owed*

their position in this country to the influence of the Court). I remember one weekend when the guests, who included the present king and queen, were entertained with an exhibition of 'stunt' shots at golf by Joe Kirkwood after lunch, with flights over the grounds in our host's private aeroplane after tea, with a firework display over the lake after dinner... and with songs by Richard Tauber, which we listened to on the Terrace by moonlight before going to bed[83].

The moonlight vanished with a finality Philip could hardly have expected. Indeed his appointment as Commissioner of Works in 1937 had crowned his political career, a public expression of his ongoing love affair with the nation's artistic heritage. Now he could exercise his own taste when refurbishing the Commons and the Royal Palaces. Yet an incipient irascibility, coupled with a deepening and inbred melancholia, was becoming more evident. Intensely superstitious – a cobra mascot was chosen for all his automobiles

[Fig 32f]
Library block under construction, refectory block in background September 1971

and aeroplanes – he seemed increasingly to court disaster. Never robust (his parents had died young) he caught influenza in the spring of 1939. The illness seems to have had a debilitating effect; in June an innocuous sore throat turned into a fatal lung infection. In retrospect he was, in Boothby's view, 'not part of England, and whatever gods he worshipped were not our Gods. Fundamentally, he was a detached and acute observer in a strange land'[84]. If that judgment sounds a mite too insular, there was, as Boothby conceded, no doubting the significance of his demise. He was the end, not only of a line but of an era. 'His death, like everything about him, was well timed'[85].

Surprisingly there was no Sassoon memorial service. Instead, in a flamboyant gesture he would have approved, his ashes were scattered over Trent Park from a plane of his Squadron 601. All the servants received one year's salary and Hannay Gubbay, cousin, hostess and last link in the Trent/Sassoon chain, became one of the principal legatees of the family fortune. Many of the treasures from the great house – thus re-establishing a link with the Earl of Cholmondeley's brief ownership of Trent Park in the eighteenth century – went to Lady Cholmondeley's (née Sybil Sassoon) seat at Houghton Hall. [Figs 18, colour plate I; 20, colour plate II; 23, colour plate III]. Exactly three months later, World War II began. The party was over not just for Philip but for his guests as well. It was closing time in the gardens of the West.

Nonetheless Sassoon's less ephemeral achievements remained – permanent testimony to the scale of his vision. It is worth summarising what he achieved at Trent. In addition to developing both the formal and wild gardens, he made five distinct contributions to the grounds. First he constructed a terrace as an interval between the house and the parkland:

> *Trent has been given the great bastion of a terrace which at once established its position in the landscape and provides a solid foundation for the house. From this plain, paved, terrace... a beautiful view is obtained northwards across the slope of the park*[86].

Secondly, he commissioned Colonel Cooper in the later 1920s to build an orangery 'in the 18th century fashion' both to accommodate the potted plants and to enclose the house architecturally to the east. Thirdly, he replaced the sunken garden between the house and this orangery (itself disguising a gravel pit) with an open air swimming pool. Fourthly, he brought Renaissance statuary from Stowe and Milton Abbey and placed it strategically around the grounds[87] [Figs 32a, p30; 32b, p33; 32c, p34]. And fifth, in 1934, he brought from Wrest Park three monuments of 18th Century Dukes of Kent in order to make Prince George and Princess Marina feel 'at home' when, as the newly-created Duke and Duchess of Kent, they spent part of their honeymoon at Trent in December 1934[88]. Novel and extravagant though these features were, they have since become part of the popular image of Trent Park.

Lord Boothby's remark about the end of an era was all too prescient. War had been in the air for some time. The inexorable march of Nazism, particularly abhorrent to someone with Sassoon's Jewish background, had been graphically brought home to him when, returning from a trip to Austria with the Windsors in 1937, he found huge swastikas on the oak gates of Trent Park. In one sense the swastika had come to stay, at least for the next few years. Plans were afoot to turn Trent Park into a prisoner-of-war camp.

IV
Trent : A Prisoner of War

As befitted its Palladian past it was no ordinary camp for POWs. Early in the war a 'Combined Services Detailed Interrogation Centre' had been created. Initially and appropriately sited at the Tower of London it was subsequently moved to Trent Park. On December 3, 1942 it was reported in the House that two German generals captured in the Western Desert were in a British POW camp. That camp was Trent Park.

If the idyllic country-house setting made these high-ranking military prisoners feel suitably privileged, then that was the unstated intention. No force was allowed but three subtler interrogation techniques were practised in the ground floor 'ante room' [Fig 10] on these potentially important informers. It was a venue not easily forgotten. Many years later, a returning German ex-officer and POW pointed excitedly to the mantelpiece in the ante-room (now the repository for staff mail) and announced 'Ah! Zat was vhere the English officer put his vhisky.' Direct questioning was the initial procedure; as soon as a prisoner showed signs of co-operating, he was offered inducements such as cigarettes if not whisky and the promise of better treatment. In many cases two interrogations, one friendly, one severe were used to the consequent disorientation of the prisoner. After all these early interrogations, prisoners were paired off in separate rooms. If they unburdened themselves to their fellow inmates, they also did so to an invisible audience. All the rooms were 'bugged' with hidden microphones. Sometimes the audience, more tangibly, was in the form of a 'mole' – an intelligence officer seeking their confidences by masquerading as a fellow German[89]. Whether all this intelligence gathering positively assisted the war effort can only be a matter for speculation. But the servants at least were convinced that the first whispers of von Braun and his V2 rockets were overheard at Trent Park.

The prisoners of war enjoyed – if that be the word – a pastoral incarceration. True, the windows of the mansion were barred and a raised cat-walk, surmounted by the inevitable barbed wire fencing encircled the great house. But the servants would watch in astonishment as twenty or even thirty prisoners would stroll round the estate accompanied by a solitary guard. In later summer and autumn, they would quarter the woods in search of edible fungi – beefsteak on the dead trees, blewits, boletuses or mushrooms in the clearings. A pleasant supplement to an austerity diet. It is amusing to contemplate the present incumbents of Trent Park who ritualistically search the parkland every autumn. They are also after mushrooms – though for a very different purpose.

Not that these distinguished house guests ever escaped – despite the latitude they were shown. Years later a film, *The One That Got Away*, was shot on location at Trent Park, but the reality was more mundane than the filmed fiction. In any case a nocturnal escape would have been difficult. Not only were the windows barred and the mansion encircled. At night the whole edifice was floodlit, a matter which caused some local residents to complain until it was pointed out that the likelihood of the Germans bombing a floodlit site was remote. Nonetheless the splendid patterned stonework of the forecourt was completely covered over with sand, because it was darkly rumoured, its resemblance to a massive Union Jack was an incitement to the enemy's bombers.

The only remaining link with an inter-war past of glitterati and glamour was now provided by Hannah Gubbay, Sassoon's cousin and hostess. She tried to maintain that connection by moving permanently into the mansion where she had hosted so many weekend events. When, however, it was requisitioned by the War Office, she was told that she would have to vacate most of the building. Not unexpectedly, Hannah Gubbay declined the 'offer' of shared accommodation and moved out to the former agent's house in the grounds. When rumours reached her that it might become an officers' mess, the beleaguered Hannah decamped, first to a flat in Brighton (where the family owned property), then a drive's-length away to a house in Cockfosters. At the end of the war she came home to what was now her estate and though in 1951 Middlesex County Council bought the entire estate by compulsory purchase order as Green Belt land, part was reserved for Mrs Gubbay during her lifetime. Now, having added a wing to both ends of the agent's cottage, she was reunited with the remarkable Sassoon collection of porcelain, paintings and furniture. Much of it had graced the reception rooms of Sir Philip's mansion; in Hannah Gubbay's cottage it found a new, if less grandiose, setting.

Even in those days the collection of furniture alone was estimated to be worth in excess of one million pounds. It was, as Mrs Gubbay came increasingly to refer to it, 'her treasure'. The collection of porcelain was said to rival the Royal Collection: certainly the Queen Mother, who visited the house two or three times a year, was a great admirer. Other visitors included Princess Alexandra and the Duke and Duchess of Kent, the latter especially fond of a place where she had spent part of her honeymoon. Hannah Gubbay, like her illustrious cousin before her, was anxious to maintain a royal family connection still inscribed on the monuments. She certainly approved the status bequeathed in the 1950s on two rooms in the mansion – one became 'The Queen Elizabeth Room' and the other 'The Princess Margaret Room'.

In the sixties, and now an old lady, Hannah Gubbay would occasionally take a slow stroll, aided by a walking-stick, round the estate. The display of daffodils in front of the mansion, still an impressive sight in mid-March, would draw her into the pallid spring sunshine. One of her favourite spots was the curved marble seat – now gone – at the secluded end of the Wistaria Walk. From there she could look down the long chiaroscuroed perspective of the pergola and recall, perhaps, elegant dresses reflected in the lily ponds or figures in plus fours golfing beyond the lake.

What she made of boisterous students passing her garden gate or splashing in her pool is impossible to say. Though she never ventured near the mansion, she was friendly to anyone willing to stop and pass the time of day. The head gardener of those days does however recall another and more mercenary side. Given bouquets by grateful house-guests, she might ask him to sell them off at market; as the donor of flowers she was liable to anticipate payment from her friends. Nonetheless Hannah Gubbay did possess an air of faded elegance, an authentic figure from a sybaritic past.

After her death in 1968 – she had survived twenty years of Trent Park's institutional life – the thousand-acre estate was divided between the London Borough of Enfield and the Greater London Council as residuary legatees of the former Middlesex County Council (which expired in 1965). For the first time since 1777, the eastern and western halves of Trent Park were divided and prepared to go their separate ways. If Hannah Gubbay had been a bit money-conscious in life, she was generous in death. Her servants were well rewarded, her 'treasure' or most of it went to the nation, her estate to all those who study here or who roam a bosky parkland no longer the preserve of the rich and titled. In time a new generation of golfers would putt on Trent Park greens. Like Sir Philip, Hannah Gubbay was not forgotten. Their names live on in the halls of residence built before her death.

V
Trent Park Renascent

By this time Trent Park's third reincarnation was well under way. For soon after the war's conclusion and the departure of its German prisoners of war, Trent Park welcomed back not only a new Hannah Gubbay but a very different kind of resident – the student teacher. Now designated as Trent Park Training College, the mansion assumed its new role in 1947. As *The Story of Trent* states:

> *The house was taken over by the Ministry of Education for use as an emergency training college for men teachers. Mr HAT Simmonds, formerly headmaster of Tottenham Grammar School, became Principal*[90].

It was a world apart from the glamour of the thirties. Nissen huts, a grim relic of the war years, still dotted the campus and were pressed into service as accommodation. As yet there were no residents, no purpose-built teaching rooms.

But the rather unhappy title of 'emergency training college' at least revealed, however baldly, the institution's new and positive role. Trent Park was to train teachers now needed in substantial numbers as a consequence of the national shortfall created by the war. Ex-servicemen would be rushed through six-month 'crash' courses at a pace unthinkable in today's world of four-year education degrees. Most of those aspiring educationists were war veterans. In an irony not lost on them, they attended lectures in the mansion, often in the same rooms where, not so long before, distinguished German officers had been interrogated.

'Hattie' Simmonds was a remarkable first principal. It is befitting that his portrait should, for many years, stare truculently down from the walls of the Senior Common Room, now the staff room. Red-faced, often puffing a cigar, he ruled his roost as a benevolent despot. Outwardly abrupt, he was nonetheless a man of humour and compassion, caring deeply for the college, and for the traditions he did so much to create. Above all he was dedicated to the students. His choice of motto, emblazoned on every student badge was 'practice before precept', appropriate for a man who was a practitioner first, a preceptor second. Yet his end-of-term addresses to the student body in the old Sports Hall (where Sir Philip Sassoon and Sir Anthony Eden had played tennis) were inspiring occasions. His students were devoted to him. He took great pleasure in walking around the campus and talking to his charges; in this way he kept abreast of student opinion.

During his tenure as principal the college flourished and burgeoned. In 1950 it became a college for men and women. One of only two colleges providing qualifications for teachers of Art, Drama and Music, Trent Park soon became nationally known for its particular strengths in these areas. Subsequently a specialist course for Handicraft teachers was initiated and a one-year course of professional training for intending secondary teachers in Music, Drama or Art of Movement. It is interesting to record that these disciplines – with 'Handicraft' metamorphosed into 'Design and Technology' and 'Art of Movement' into 'Dance' – are still studied on the same Trent Park campus of what is now Middlesex University, a tribute if one were needed, to the resilience of that creative tradition at Trent Park. It might be known as 'the Bohemian college' but it produced genuinely innovative teachers.

That these areas did give the college a significant reputation was in part a consequence of HAT Simmond's capacity for recruiting exceptional staff to lead those departments – EJ Burton, an ex-priest to run Drama; Sidney Glenister, Handicraft; Philip Pfaff, Music; Douglas Richmond, Art and Crafts. All these were people of considerable personal charisma and though they did not always see eye to eye with 'Hattie' or with each other, they ran their departments with elan. When the college opened its doors to women students and as the range of subjects increased, other tutors came to leaven the academic mix. Eric Barker, who at his untimely death, had more than sixty publications to his credit, came to build up Geography, Walter Millard to take charge of Science, Mary Lane of the library. Later on Patrick Anderson, a well-known Hellenophile and Canadian poet took charge of the English department. Alicia Percival and Miss Armstrong, the vice-principal, ran education, benevolent Rex Zissell was senior tutor. In general the academic staff did not move on elsewhere, though Leonard Bewsher subsequently became principal of Cardiff College of Education and at least two tutors defected to the greyer pastures of the University of London Institute of Education. To read the roll-call of all those fifties and early sixties names is to reanimate the spirit of Trent Park in those far-off days.

In 1962 'Hattie' Simmonds retired. His successor, TE Theakston, inherited a flourishing institution. A mathematician who had trained at the College of St Mark and St John in Chelsea, Thomas Theakston, had served in the Royal Air Force – an irony that would not have been lost on Sassoon. He had then been appointed to the staff of Cowley Emergency College at Coventry as a lecturer. Later Head of the Mathematics department at Coventry Training College, he came to Trent Park with a considerable reputation in the area of mathematical education, having developed a large department before becoming second deputy principal at Coventry.

When Thomas Theakston arrived, Trent Park was a small but well known college, its 'arty' ambience very different from the new principal's previous institution. Nonetheless he oversaw Trent Park's development during his twelve years of stewardship into one of the largest colleges in the country. His arrival, as Alison Grady, later his deputy principal recalls, 'coincided with the introduction of the three-year course and the national plan for rapid expansion of the colleges of education'[91]. Let her take up the story:

> *At Trent Park he devoted himself to the development of a very different type of college, one established in a beautiful parkland environment and specializing in teacher education and the arts. He.... consistently maintained this emphasis so that, despite the advancement of other studies to a high level, Trent Park retained its prominence in the arts. Schools, children and professional preparation remain central to the college life and work*[92].

Expansion was a reiterated educational theme in the sixties and seventies. Trent Park, with its obvious physical capacity for growth, outstripped national trends; with the student body growing so rapidly it became necessary to undertake an ambitious building programme. As a first stage two halls of residence were built in 1964 on the 'campus' (a term used at Trent Park long before it became fashionable parlance). One, the Hannah Gubbay Hall, which overlooks the privet hedge of the Gubbay garden, still pays homage to Sir Philip's hostess and cousin who had continued to live in the dower house until her death in 1968.

These residences – the other beyond the stable yard that had once housed his polo ponies and their grooms was fittingly called Philip Sassoon Hall – introduced an incongruous architectural note. Nonetheless, in practical if not in aesthetic terms they were welcomed, for they made Trent Park a genuinely residential college for the first time. Previous generations of students had found living in the suburbs of Oakwood and Cockfosters a financially daunting experience. Now Gubbay Hall, built in a buff brick that at least blended with the Stable Yard's muted colours, could accommodate two hundred women students, each with her own study bedroom. Sassoon Hall, smaller and lower, was for forty men. While the practice of segregating sexes has long since been abandoned – it was first questioned during the student uprisings of 1968 – it is interesting to note that the initial idea of giving residential preference to first-year undergraduates is still a cornerstone of university policy.

Beyond the Cockfosters Gate and down Chalk Lane past 'The Cock' – now 'The Cock and Dragon' – public house, was another student residence of a quite different character, Ludgrove Hall. Originally a well-known 'prep' school, which numbered among its alumni Winston Churchill, it did at one time apparently include a reluctant John Betjeman on its staff. In his poem 'Cricket Master', he recalls a Georgian idyll of 'narrow lanes... between the dairy farms' and 'three halves for me' 'on the wooden bench outside The Cock' before the sterner business of the 'Parents' Match'[93].

Physically distanced from the changing Trent Park environment, Ludgrove Hall still wore a pastoral air, its fine grounds close to Hadley Woods apparently little changed by thirty years of progress. The male students who came to live there, shared large study bedrooms and took pride in traditions that seemed to harp back to its 'prep' school past. Every evening, there was formal dinner at seven o'clock in the hall, at which Latin grace was said. Woe betide any student who arrived late or tieless.

It has always been a matter of surprise to me – as to others – that Trent Park has been so little used as a location by film makers.

Apart from *The One That Got Away*, only one feature film has exploited what is, undeniably, a most photogenic locale. One chill spring morning in 1967 staff arrived to find a swimming pool misty with steaming vapours and glowing with flowery islets of water lilies. Ivy, miraculously venerable, draped itself over the walls of the orangery. That evening most of the student body stayed up to watch the night-long shooting of scenes from a Michael Winner movie that was later given the unconvincing title of *I'll Never Forget What's 'Is Name*. The orangery and blue-rinsed pool were eerily floodlit, Michael Winner bellowed directorially through a megaphone at crinolined ladies on the orangery steps, Orson Welles emerged moodily from his haven in the Blue Room to confront the cameras, and Carol White swam pallidly among the lilies. In the way of these things not everything went according to plan. Oliver Reed, required in a moment of unbridled passion, to leap from the terrace to the pool side, missed the mattress intended as cushion for his bulky frame and reappeared, swearing audibly and covered in mud. After the conclusion of filming, the director complained to the college authorities that most of his plastic water lilies had vanished – as mysteriously it seemed as they had arrived: a quick check revealed that they had left their element for student rooms in Gubbay Hall. But the college, it was rumoured, benefited to the princely tune of fifty pounds for playing host to Mr Winner and his stars...

On the campus other changes of a less emphemeral and spectacular kind were in the offing. The mansion, long the hub of the college life, was still the focal point, with administration on the ground floor and teaching on the first and second floors. The Blue Room, with its Rex Whistler murals remained as the Senior Common Room, the library still occupied the Saloon and Drawing Room that overlooked the terrace and commanded the picturesque vista beyond. There, boasted the college prospectus of 1965, were '15,000 books... added to at the rate of some 1,000 volumes a year as it is the college policy to acquire a stock gradually and so keep in touch with contemporary trends'[94]. Rooms in which dolphins yet spouted above the bookshelves or birds peered from the Chinese wallpaper now echoed, not to the tinkle of champagne flutes and animated laughter but to the subdued rustle of turning pages.

But new buildings were needed and new buildings began to appear beyond the confines of the mansion and its splendid forecourt, now no longer a potential target for German bombs but a staff car park. To the west of the mansion, in a move which destroyed at a stroke the symmetry that Sir Philip had sought to impose, a new teaching block was erected together with a large assembly hall with a fully equipped stage. Adjoining the theatre was a stagecraft room, lighting and make-up rooms. Beyond the hall was a large gymnasium. There were science laboratories for the general science course, fully equipped maths and geography rooms on the first floor and the sound of music filtered down from the second floor of the new building where there was a large space for orchestral work and no fewer than twenty practice cells. Above the new refectory, a college lecture room was built for the large groups that were now required to be taught. Each subject head was given a tutorial room; lesser mortals still had to share rooms.

The stable yard, in pre-war days the home of Sassoon's polo ponies, had also undergone considerable internal reconstruction and renovation – though the character of the low quadrangle of buildings, surmounted by its unassuming clock tower and cupola, was mercifully retained. Now devoted mainly to art, it had two rooms for painting, an art and craft room, a pottery room and a needlecraft room. 'Queen Elizabeth's Room', so named after a visit by her Royal Highness to the mansion in the fifties, was no longer the preserve of needlecraft. By the same token 'The Princess Margaret Room', so named after a royal visit in 1958, lost its affiliations with drama. The rest of the stable yard became the preserve of handicraft with metalwork facilities, a technical drawing room and, across the road in the old refectory, advanced and elementary woodwork rooms.

The next building stage was completed in 1973. [Figs 32d, p37; 32e, p38; 32f, p39]. The college prospectus for that year describes the additions in the following terms:

> *A major building project recently completed provides a new dining hall, library and study accommodation, specialist teaching areas for music, art, craft and design, education and a student union building*[95].

The changes were indeed considerable though both the siting and style of the buildings attracted some adverse criticism. The Music Centre, which abutted the rear of the orangery, cut right across the old perspectives of the long border and though four of the lily ponds were preserved, the 'rond point' and, much of the formal yew hedging succumbed to the bulldozer. Beyond, a large new block accommodated 'Craft and Design' and 'Art and Craft', now evacuated from the stable yard. Further east a substantial refectory was built, along with housing for domestic staff.

The most contentious development concerned the siting of the new library and hall. Originally intended for the car park area, it was decided, by the Enfield architect responsible for the designs, to reposition the new building on the lakeside lawns. Placed to the left of 'Repton's' landscape, its positioning effectively obliterated the picturesque vista linking terrace, lake and water garden. Moreover its flat bituminous roof was all too visible from the elevated rooms of the mansion on the north side. "A blot on the landscape" in the opinion of many academic staff and local conservationists, the tutorial staff had been refused access to the campus during the Easter vacation while the foundations were laid. Nonetheless the library block, with its all-purpose hall and tutorial rooms as well as a library now unrivalled for its video collection of live arts material, has served the college community in good stead, despite it unlovely appearance and positioning. And it gave rise to the birth of a powerful conservationist lobby in the college community, which, in the form of a committee is to this day strenuously pledged to protect the aesthetic values and traditions of Trent Park. 'It's an ill wind...'

But even greater changes were presaged that year. If the new building programme had attracted mixed reviews, the proposal to join Middlesex Polytechnic was greeted by some with a scepticism that bordered on hostility. The college prospectus inevitably put the matter more blandly:

> *At the time of going to press (May 1973) the college governors have approved a proposal that the college should begin negotiating with a view to integrating with the Middlesex Polytechnic. These proposals need the approval both of Enfield LEA and the DES, but if they go through, the whole structure and status of the college will change in the next academic year. There are likely to be enlarged opportunities for students though courses are not likely to change fundamentally for those entering in September 1974*[96].

This proposed amalgamation reflected what was going on up and down the country. Thirty polytechnics had been proposed in a White Paper of May 1966 *(A Plan for*

Polytechnics and Other Colleges); they were to be formed from existing institutions already engaged in higher education. Broad-based and innovatory in course design, they were pledged to the development of new types of interdisciplinary and modular degree courses and to the recruitment of students with diverse backgrounds and interests.

Middlesex, the twenty-ninth polytechnic to be designated, had already embraced the former Enfield and Hendon Colleges of Technology and Hornsey College of Art. On 1 September 1974 and after protracted discussions, Trent Park College along with New College of Speech and Drama (Ivy House) joined the new institution. Though many staff had reservations about the move and forcibly expressed them to the Governing Body and Raymond (later Sir Raymond) Rickett, the new director, they probably knew that Trent Park could not survive as an autonomous entity. Such institutions were becoming anachronistic. The time was right in other ways. Thomas Theakston had retired, his last years as principal – the years of international student unrest – more fraught than he would have hoped. Alison Grady, his deputy, was ready and able to attend to the complicated processes that were occasioned by the merger. Moreover the demand for teachers had ebbed away and the estimates of teachers required in future underwent a drastic downward revision. It was time for Trent Park to broaden its educational provision.

It is not the purpose of this account to consider the overall operation of Middlesex Polytechnic except in so far as it relates to Trent Park. And so much change was in the air in 1974, it is difficult to recall the fine detail twenty years on. Suffice to say that the new polytechnic began life on fifteen sites (Bounds Green was soon added) and with a commitment to 150 discrete courses. It operated what its scientist director was pleased to call a 'matrix' form of academic administration with 'courses' on one side and 'resource centres' on the other. There were six faculties – Art and Design, Business Studies, Education and Performing Arts, Engineering and Science, Humanities, and Social Science. Rapid growth was anticipated. Projected student numbers were expected to reach over 8,000 by 1981.

Amidst all this change, Trent Park retained its position as a centre for education and the performing arts. The new faculty's title acknowledged this academic emphasis. The BEd degree, now no longer affiliated to University of London Institute of Education, remained the staple offering – the James report of 1971 had advocated the notion of an all-graduate teaching profession – but plans were afoot to develop a BA in Performance Arts which would draw on the long established strengths of the college in the areas of drama, dance and music. It was intended as a more integrated degree course with a strong interdisciplinary emphasis. In 1975 the BA in Performance Arts, together with the new Bachelor of Education degree, were submitted for approval to the Council for National Academic Awards, the body now responsible for ratifying new courses developed by the polytechnics. The BAPA was the first degree of its kind in the country to gain approval.

By 1977 Middlesex was developing apace. Another substantial innovative course was in the process of being established, a trail-blazing modular course that heralded a trans-Atlantic and unitised approach to higher education. Called, in its initial form, the Diploma of Higher Education, the course was designed to cater, as befitted the institution's avowed aims, to a wide range of student interests and to draw on a broad spectrum of student backgrounds. It offered participants the opportunity to build up their own programmes of study from a constantly growing list of disciplines and course units. Ten years after its inception the Modular Degree Scheme embraced thirty subject sets with over four hundred course modules and had proved its worth in attracting the part-time and mature students who might otherwise have missed the opportunity to study to degree level. Its principles and procedures now dominate the institution's academic provision.

Amidst all this expansion, Trent Park retained its pivotal position. No longer the largest campus in terms of numbers, it was still the hub of operations. Sir Raymond Rickett had his office in the mansion – with enviable views of the 'Repton' landscape and orangery – while his residence, as it has been for subsequent vice-chancellors, was the former dower house of Hannah Gubbay – the current occupant being Professor Michael Driscoll appointed 1 October 1996. It was generally Trent Park – the jewel in the crown – that distinguished academic visitors saw rather than other polytechnic sites of less prepossessing appearance, Trent Park that dominated Middlesex brochures and prospectuses. For courses in the performing arts it remained an ideal location in an idyllic setting.

VI
Trent : Campus and Country Park

In March 1991, Sir Raymond Rickett retired after guiding the Polytechnic through its first eighteen years. The figure of eighteen augured well for the institution; in one sense at least it had come of age. Awarded a knighthood in the previous year, Sir Raymond had already received many accolades in recognition of his distinctive contribution to higher education. In a valedictory interview with Mike Brown of *North Circular* (the polytechnic's weekly newspaper), he expounded on his stewardship in terms of his stated priorities of 'wider participation', 'credit transfer' and international links. A man who attributed his iconoclasm to working-class roots, he had, he explained, consistently campaigned against 'entrenched positions': the dominance of the established and traditional universities, single honours system, inequitable funding mechanisms. Middlesex had, he averred, 'in many areas blazed a trail which others followed'[97].

Others were now to follow in his footsteps. The appointment of a new director – not long in coming – was ratified by the governors on 7 May. Professor David Melville, vice-rector of Lancashire Polytechnic and possessor of a distinguished academic record, was the new appointee.

Within a year and even before the new director had had time to settle into the dower house so recently vacated by Sir Raymond, the name Middlesex Polytechnic had ceased to exist. David Melville became the main player in a metamorphosis whereby Middlesex, anticipating major changes proposed for higher education, became a university. Events moved rapidly to a conclusion. As the *Barnet and Finchley Press* reported on 14 May 1992:

> *After twenty years as one of the largest polytechnics in the country, the newly constituted university assumed its identity in a series of ceremonies at its main locations last Wednesday. The main ceremony took place at the university's Trent Park site in Cockfosters where hundreds of staff and students watched the Vice-Chancellor, Professor David Melville, symbolically raise the new flag*[99].

At the ceremony, as a response to the reforms of the Further and Higher Education Act, the new Vice-Chancellor remarked:

> *It recognises something we have known for some time – that polytechnics are universities. We are taking the step of assuming our university identity early – in this it is our intention to maintain Middlesex University at the forefront of higher education.*

Warming to his theme, he added:

> *In being recognised as a university I would like to confirm our commitment to high quality higher education, to access for mature students from a wide range of backgrounds and cultures; to confirm our commitment to our local community in offering the widest possible range of courses, flexible modes of study, research at the leading edge and consultancy for industry and commerce*[100].

Benefiting from a broader philosophy in terms of higher education, community service, committed to the notion of equal status with traditional universities, Middlesex would thus be in a position to increase student numbers to well over 20,000 before the turn of the century – double the figure in 1991. Already, by 1994, this prognosis showed every prospect of being fulfilled: 16,800 students were enrolled on courses at the university.

It is not the primary purpose of this brief account to focus on the whole institution – after all this is a history of Trent Park – but some sense of the changes which went on in the wider context of the university at large do help to put the Trent Park story in perspective. Certainly the siting of the principal naming ceremony at Trent Park reflected both the primacy of its performing arts traditions and its central role in the future life of the institution. In a felicitous gesture that forged anew the Jewish connection, fourteen fiddlers from the university's School of Music played 'Fiddler on the Roof' atop the mansion as the Vice-Chancellor raised the flag of Middlesex University, its fast-forward logo emblazoned in red and black. A month later, the title of Middlesex University was formally conferred by Privy Council. Another page in the Trent Park story had been turned, another chapter begun.

If the university was now committed to matters of academic excellence and innovation that required a concentration on an exciting present and expansionist future, it was not about to forget those aspects of its past worth memorialising. As the hub of the new empire, Trent Park merited some care and attention.

As I write, two years on, Trent Park is being restored not to its former thirties country house state – after all this is a thriving university campus for 3,000 or so students – but to a standard that everywhere reveals a concern for its traditions and its enduring aesthetic appeal. This is due, in large measure, to the untiring efforts of the Conservation Committee, chaired ever since its inception by Douglas Dawson, and to the commitment of Professor David Melville, who, during his tenancy as Vice-Chancellor took an interest in the past, present and future of Trent Park. His successor Professor Michael Driscoll has also been actively involved in negotiating planning approvals and the implementation of a comprehensive masterplan for the development of the university campus area. Because the Conservation Committee has been such a positive force for good in this process, a short summary of its activities is appropriate.

Most important of all these has been its pivotal role in monitoring unsuitable building projects and ensuring that the unique 'feel' of Trent Park is retained. It played a crucial part in blocking Enfield's application to Parliament - after the death of Hannah Gubbay - for a revision of the Green Belts Act that would have meant a rash of housing on Trent Park. That a Conservation Order protects the mansion, its decorative forecourt and the clock house area is also thanks to a TPCC which gained a voice once it was formally co-opted on to the Enfield Council's Conservation Advisory Group. The committee has quietly and effectively gone about its business for twenty-five years - planting specimen and memorial trees, replanting daffodils, twice restoring the pergola, cleaning the statuary, negotiating the renovation of the once-doomed Chinese wallpapers, setting up an archive collection, ensuring the listing and grading of the main buildings[101].

The visible benefits are everywhere in evidence. Today rows of apple trees remain in the walled garden to remind the curious student of the exotic fruit trees and espaliers that once flourished there. The grassy slopes fore and aft of the mansion, once allowed to run to seed, are now cut and manicured; visitors can again admire the Easter parade of daffodils that 'come before the swallow dares'[102]. Even the muntjack deer, residents on the estate since the 1920s are now protected, as are the great crested grebes which patrol the central reaches of the upper lake. In the ornamental trees that share the same grassy area, the history of Trent's recent past is writ large - green memorials to staff and students whose contributions to the life of Trent Park are thus remembered. Of these the oldest and most impressive is the red-leaved 'quercus' which casts its shadow into the Blue Room, a reminder of the incumbency of 'Hattie' Simmonds as first principal. A few yards up the slope, a sapling oak, dwarfed by the venerable specimen in the centre of the green, carries an inscription 'To the memory of Rex Zissell, senior tutor from 1947-1967'. Towards the lily ponds, another 'quercus' hallows the memory of Wilfred MacKenzie, warden of Ludgrove Hall.

Though some of the smaller and more portable eighteenth century pieces from Stowe and Milton Abbey have gone (some apparently removed by zealous builders never to reappear), the sphinxes which guard the terrace steps remain, along with the huge baroque statues of wrestling combatants below the terracing formerly aligned with the 'road point'. So too the familiar landmarks on the Cockfosters Drive [Fig 33, p56]. Now restored, the accumulated grime of fifty years has been erased to reveal stonework of a rich cream. Visitors approaching from the Cockfosters gate may dally for a moment to read the inscription on the obelisk that marks the beginning of the straight carriageway, a monument not only to Sir Philip's aesthetic sense but above all to his willingness to go to any lengths to make the honeymooning Kents feel at home in 1934 [Fig 33, p56]. For it reads 'To the Memory of Henry, Duke of Kent' and is adorned with the family motto *Honi Soit Qui Mal y Pense*. At the mansion end, the cylindrical column dedicated 'To the Memory of Emma Crewe, Dutchess [sic] of Kent' - surmounted by a pineapple and thus known to generations of students - now gleams with rediscovered whiteness as, sentinel

[Fig 33]
Trent Park:
Cockfosters drive
today

like, it guards the approach to the mansion [Fig 32a, p30]. The pergola, above the long border, all too long in a condition of ruinous neglect has also been restored, its 26 pink columns once more harmonising with the violet racemes of May-blooming wistaria [Fig27, p25]. Unlatch the black wrought iron gates at the long border end and re-enter a Georgian world where a strolling house guest, even a pensive Sir Philip, would hardly seem out of place.

Beyond the university campus, the surrounding estate is in good hands. The storms of 1987 played havoc with the birches in the bluebell woods near the pineapple, tore huge limbs from the mansion cedars and felled massive oaks in the parkland abutting the Cockfosters drive. More than a thousand trees were lost. But man and nature in her benevolent mood, working in harmony, have restored the lineaments of the landscape. The conifers planted on the golf course are reaching maturity, the woods of the chase, now accessible to the walkers who follow the signposted paths are responding to the care of the Enfield Leisure Services. Even the eyesore of open-cast excavations beyond the lake, decreed by a European Union directive, and gouged, quite inappropriately, on the very site of Sir Philip's nine-hole golf course, are now healing. The lake, dredged and refilled, again has its native complement of coot, moorhen and mallard; flocks of geese honk and hiss at the unwary walker. The water garden has been refurbished with azaleas and magnolias, maple and eucalyptus trees. Flags and kingcups reflect yellow in the lily ponds; even if the stands of lilium giganteum have not reappeared, a gunnera adds an exotic touch that Sir Philip would have approved.

It is difficult to assess Sir Philip's enthusiasm for the more rustic aspects of his parkland estate; he was not, after all, obliged to show any concern either for nature or human nature save when such matters impinged directly on his consciousness or that of his guests. But the Greater London Council, which opened 413 acres of the park to the public in 1973, and more recently Enfield Leisure Services have, of necessity, been more conservation minded. Coppicing and replanting schemes have ensured the continuing character of the ancient woodlands such as Oak Wood. William's Wood, a mature pine afforestation has been turned into mixed woodland by broadleaf plantings. Wild flowers have been reintroduced to parts of the parkland, nesting rafts have been provided for waders and hedgerow planting schemes based on blackthorn and hawthorn are intended to encourage smaller birds. Nor has human nature been neglected. The public golf course has proved a successful venture and the cafeteria, discreetly placed amid the trees of Oak Wood in 1982 has proved both an effective marketing device and source of income. The Walk for the Blind, which now boasts a tapping rail is conveniently close at hand and the park's bike trail, opened in 1993, features open grassland riding with woodland stretches, stream crossings and a trail indicated by waymarks on posts. The lakes, now dredged, are to be managed by a club so that the general public can once again enjoy fishing for pike or roach.

The buildings of Trent Park, many renamed, now genuflect suitably to the past. Unlovely and all too functional names have been changed. The 'Mansion Extension' is now the Sir Richard Jebb building, testimony to George III's miracle-cure physician who between the years of 1777 and 1787 created the original house and landscaped the park. 'B Block' – reminiscent of Trent's prison past – is now named after the Bevan family who owned the estate for much of the nineteenth century. The impressive ground floor suite of rooms ('a suite of three principal saloons superbly decorated at great expense' said a sale notice in *The Times* of August, 1807) and which Sir Philip subsequently made a focal point for his soirées are still there, features not only preserved but recently repainted in appropriate colours which show a proper concern for their arcadian past. Whistler's dolphins still pout and spout over the lintel of the Venetian window; at the other end, his Greek warrior women, hunting horns poised and shields emblazoned with Sir Philip's initials still confront each other above the Boardroom shelves. Next door, most of the Chinese wallpaper with its delicate birds amid the blossom, has survived the comings and goings of prisoners, students and tutors for over half a century. Take the Kent staircase, its oak panels and balusters newly restored, to the landing above where the Vice-Chancellor now controls his university empire from a suite of rooms on the first floor. It is an inspiring setting in which to work. To the north are the 'picturesque' vistas of the lake and the spinneys of the Chase beyond. To the south is a bustling microcosmos, a university campus indubitably but also a place pastoral enough, especially in high summer, to make one forget that all this is a mere twelve miles from the West End of London.

If the story has in recent decades necessarily tended to accentuate the divide between town and gown, between 'private' campus initiative and 'public' parkland re-development, at least one innovation has happily brought the local and academic communities closer together and, recreated a midsummer festival in which man and nature combine to splendid effect. This is the series of fireworks concerts introduced by the university in 1993, successfully repeated in June of 1994 and 1995, and now happily envisaged as an annual event. Featuring a full symphony orchestra of 60 players, and culminating on each of three nights with a pyrotechnical display, it is a mix of sound and spectacle, of son et lumière in a lakeside setting that is set fair to rival the Kenwood

[Fig 34b]
Prince Edward is greeted by David Peacock for the Royal Gala performance of *Man of La Mancha*, June 1990.

[Fig 36]
The young family, by Zoffany. The Dining Room, Trent Park, 1931

concerts on Hampstead Heath. Thousands picnic on the grassy slopes betwixt Sassoon's terracing and Repton's lake, entertained on a scale reminiscent of Trent's thirties spectaculars but all the better for being enjoyed by local people [Fig 34a, colour plate IV].

Moreover, the royal connection, originally established during the first years of Sassoon's incumbency, has been forged anew. On 21 June 1990, Prince Edward attended the Royal Gala performance of *Man of La Mancha* in the Simmonds Theatre at Trent Park [Fig 34b, p58]. Directed by the university's principal lecturer in music David Peacock, the event provided evidence of a thriving artistic tradition – that of the summer musical – but marked the reassertion of a royal link that had begun with George III's grateful gift

[Fig 37]
A corner of the Blue Room at Trent Park, 1931

of land to Richard Jebb and carried on in the twentieth century with the inter-war visits of the Windsors and Kents, the postwar appearance of the Queen, and the friendship of the Queen Mother with Hannah Gubbay. History has a habit of repeating itself...

One coda to the story of Trent Park is of yet more recent provenance. On Thursday 8 December 1994, a massive sale of works of art from Houghton Hall took place at Christie's. It was an event not without its sadness. For in 1991, the Marchioness of Cholmondeley had passed away, the last close tie with Sir Philip sundered by the death of an only sister whose youthful beauty, he once averred, had prevented him from marrying. Many of Sassoon's objets d'art from Trent Park had, unsurprisingly, ended up at Houghton Hall, a suitably baronial setting for items from a magnificent and unique collection. Now it was being auctioned off, and one's delight in recognising so many treasures from the 1931 photographs of the Trent Park drawing rooms, library and saloon, was tempered by the realisation that the collection was being broken up and passing out of the family's hands [Figs 35, colour plate IV; 36, p59; 37, p60].

Nonetheless the sale provided additional evidence – if evidence be needed – both of Sir Philip's impeccable and very English tastes – particularly in Georgian japanned furniture, and of a still buoyant market for unique 'objets d'art', a uniqueness demonstrated by the splendid full-plate photographs in the Christie's catalogue [Fig 38, colour plate V]. Two matching Queen Anne pieces – a pair of scarlet and gilt-japanned pier glasses and a dressing table, and now auctioned off as separate lots, realised £370,000. Sold along with an 18th-century Portuguese Armorial carpet (£28,000), they represented just some of the red furnishings in the Blue Room of the 1930s [Figs 39, colour plate VI; 40, colour plate VII]. A pair of George II gilt and marble side tables that had graced the Saloon went for £110,000. Also in the sale were a lacquer and gilt screen from the dining (Green) room, George III lacquer and satinwood bookcases from the library, a black and gilt secretaire from Sir Philip's bedroom and Georgian chairs and stools from the dining room and corridor. Interestingly, furniture from all the main rooms at Trent Park came under the auctioneer's hammer[103].

But it would be wrong to end on an elegiac or mercenary note.

After all, Trent Park has undergone many moults and seen many changes since John Evelyn described its parkland in 1676 as a 'solitary desert' inhabited only by deer[104]. It enjoyed one heyday in Sassoon's time; now it enjoys another, its delights no longer available to the country-house set of prewar England, but to a new generation of music lovers, golfers, walkers, teachers and above all students who for three formative years can enjoy the privilege of working, playing and creating in unique surroundings. The History of Trent Park is still being written.

[Fig 41a]
Ludgrove Hall, 1983
(Middlesex University
Conference Centre
until 1996)

[Fig 41b]
Ludgrove Hall
(aerial view), 1982

VII
Notes

Abbreviations:

DL Duchy of Lancaster

PRO Public Record Office

Harl Harleian

1. This chapter has been reprinted, with only minor corrections, from the original 1974 edition of *Trent Park, A Short History to 1939*. The most authoritative work on all aspects of the history of Enfield Chase is DO Pam, *The Story of Enfield Chase* (Enfield, 1984)

2. *The Diary of John Evelyn*, ed ES de Beer (1959) p626

3. In the light of David Pam's researches, the identification of Enfield Chase with the Domesday park at Enfield is unlikely, see Pam, op cit p11

4. PRO DL42/18f, Duchy of Lancaster warrant, 3 May 1440

5. 'The Middlesex Domesday', in *The Victoria County History of Middlesex*, i (1969) p126b

6. See *Curia Rolls of the Reign of Henry III* (1961) xiv, No 1644, p350 for an early case of illegal hunting in Enfield Park

7. This map is reproduced in Pam, op cit p71. See also GH Hodsdon and E Ford, *History of Enfield* (Enfield) 1873.

8. N Salmon, *History of Hertfordshire*, 1728 p55

9. DO Pam, *The Fight for Common Rights in Enfield and Edmonton*, 1400-1600 (Edmonton Hundred Historical Society, Occasional Papers NS, 27)

10. BL Harl MS 570, f13; John Norden's Notes on Middlesex

11. Robinson, op cit i, 196 note 1; *Calendar of State Papers Domestic* (Henceforth referred to as CSPD) 1637-38, p487

12. CSPD 1649-50, pp192 and 392; 1650 p414

13. CSPD 1654, pp341-2, 30 Aug 1654. The Council of State ordered a new survey to be made on 10 June 1656, CSPD 1655-56, p364.

14. CSPD 1659, p363

15. CSPD 1660, p394, No 153

16. D Defoe, *A Tour Through the Whole Island of Great Britain*, 1724-26 (1962 ed) ii, 3

17. PRO DL 41/16/12: Memorial of John Pepper to the Chancellor of the Duchy of Lancaster, 1716

18. Thomas Fuller, *The Worthies of England* (1662) sub 'Hertfordshire'

19. A Young, *A Six Months' Tour of the Northern Counties* (1770) iv, 29

20. An Act for Dividing the Chace of Enfield in the County of Middlesex 27 March, 1777

21. A map of the allotments is reproduced in DO Pam, op cit p150 and in N Clarke, *Hadley Wood* (1968) facing p126

22. L Middleton, *View of the Agriculture of Middlesex* (1798), p118 and Appendix 5, pp S22-3

23 *Dictionary of National Biography*, x, 699-700; W.Munk, *The Roll of the Royal College of Physicians, 1701-1800* (1878), p292; 'GEC', *Complete Peerage*, (1906) v, 206

24 *The last Journals of Horace Walpole...from 1771 to 1783*, (ed AF Steuart, 1910), i, 205, 445, 505, 525; ii, 38, 51-55; V Biddulph, T (1938), 0121

25 PRO DL 42/168, pp27-332: Enrolment of leases, Duchy of Lancaster

26 Sir John Soane's Museum, Reveley Drawings, AL/8C/21; J Harris, *Sir William Chambers* (1970), plate 74

27 Enfield Library

28 *Gentleman's Magazine*, 1787, pp643 and 834

29 Ibid p834

30 *Country Life*, 10 January 1931, p40

31 PRO DL 42/168/34 (1787); 42/169/14 (1793); 42/171/4 (1810)

32 Middleston, op cit., App 10, p153: letter of J Wigston, 8 Sept 1796

32a In *The Ambulator*, a publication of 1800 which purported to describe 'whatever is most remarkable for Antiquity, Grandeur, Elegance, or Rural Beauty' within ....twenty-five miles .... of the Metropolis', Trent Place was referred to as 'a beautiful villa on Enfield Chase'. Erected, the writer suggested 'in imitation of an Italian loggia', it contained 'a music-room' and was set in what was now 'a delightful park'.

33 Engraving of Trent Place by Sturt, 27 Feb 1808, published in Hughson, *Circuit of London* (1809), p405; engraving of Trent Place by H Hobson, 1 July 1815, published in JN Brewer, *Beauties of Middlesex* (1816), p735

34 *The Times* 8 August 1807, p4

35 PRO DL 42/171, pp252-61: assignment of lease to John Cumming, 30 January 1813. This deed also casts light on the Lushington bankruptcy.

36 Bewer, op cit p734

37 'Ambulator', *The Stranger's Guide, or the New Ambulator* (1825), p278

38 Sale notices in *The Times*, 29 October and 4 December 1832. I am indebted to Mr Clive Fleay for this reference.

39 Book of Patents, Duchy of Lancaster Office, lancaster Place (oral information)

40 The assignment of the lease to David Bevan is dated 19 May 1833, ibid; AN Gamble, *A History of the Bevan Family* (1924) p123

41 W Keane, *The Beauties of Middlesex* (1850), pp154-6

42 GH Hodson and E Ford, *History of Enfield* (Enfield, 1873), facing p53

43 N Webster, *Spacious Days* (1950), opposite p49

44 Ibid, opposite p49

45 Robert Bevan died in July 1890

46 10 Feb 1893 (oral information, Duchy of Lancaster Office). See also A McKenzie, 'The Trent Park Oak', *Hertfordshire Illustrated Review*, ii (1989), 11

47 *Country Life*, 27 Feb 1903, pp240-6

48 Ibid, p246

49 O Sitwell, *The Scarlet Tree* (1946) p132

50 Lady Cynthia Asquith, *Diaries, 1915-18* (1968), p60

51 'Almost every cottage on the estate had been rebuilt during Mr Bevan's residence there', *Meyer's Enfield Observer*, 15 Feb 1889, p6

52 The assignment is dated 1 December 1908, enrolment of leases, Duchy of Lancaster Office

53 Stanley Jackson, *The Sassoons* (1968) p39

53a Later on number 45 Park Lane (the numbering was changed during the 1930s). After the war the building was demolished. 'The panelling from the Palais Paar was sold to the Wrightsman collection and the Sert murals (in the ballroom) were acquired by the Museum of Modern Art in Barcelona' (Christie's Houghton catalogue p26). Subsequently a new structure erected in concrete on the site became the Playboy Club. At the time of writing number 45 is owned by a Japanese consortium.

54 C Roth, *The Sassoon Dynasty* (1941) p234

55 S Jackson, p132

56 Ibid, pp 144-145

57 Siegfried Sassoon, 'Base Details' (4 March 1917) in *Collected Poems* (1984) p75

58 C Roth, p246

59 S Jackson p146

60 C Roth, p272

61 Siegfried Sassoon, *Letters to Max Beerbohm* (ed) R Hart-Davis (1986) p47

62 Many of these furnishings, paintings and art objects found their way to Houghton Hall after Sir Philip's death in 1939. A substantial number of these including the celebrated painting by Jean-François de Troy – *La Lecture de Molière* – were sold at Christie's on 8 December 1994 in what was dubbed, 'The Sale of the Decade'. Sybil, 5th Marchioness of Cholmondeley and Sassoon's sister, had died in 1991. See Christie's catalogue, *Works of Art from Houghton*, for further details concerning these items and their provenance.

63 S Sassoon, 'Monody on the Demolition of Devonshire House', in *Collected Poems* (1984) p131

64 *Country Life*, 10 January (1931) pp40-47 and 17 January 1931 pp66-72. The articles are the major sources for Sassoon's rebuilding of Trent Park. Neither gives the name of the architect. (SD)

65 Ibid, p44

66 Ibid, p68

67 Ibid, p66

68 Ibid, p70

69 S Sassoon 'Monody on the Demolition of Devonshire House'.

70 Alec Dale, head gardener at Trent Park. Oral information

71 *Trent: A Descriptive Guide to the Gardens*, (privately published in the 1930s) p10

72 Alec Dale, head gardener. Oral information

73 Robert Boothby, *I Fight to Live* (1947) p49

74 Alec Dale. Oral information

75 S Jackson, *The Sassoons* (1968) p188

76 Alec Dale. Oral information

77 S Jackson, p188

78 Ibid, p188

79 C Roth, *The Sassoon Dynasty* (1941) p247

80 S Jackson, p221

81 Ibid, p221

82 Portrait by John Sargent (c1912) Tate Gallery

83 R Boothby, p49

84 Ibid, p48

85 Ibid, p51

86 *Trent: A Descriptive Guide to the Gardens* p3

87 Ibid, p3; *Enfield Gazette and Observer*, 9 June 1939, p20

88 *The Times* 13 December 1934, p16

89 Richard Garrett, *POW* (1981) p165

90 Winifred Walles, *The Story of Trent* (privately printed 1958) p9

91 *Trent Park Essays* (ed) D J Ellis, (privately printed 1974) p1

92 Ibid, p2

93 John Betjeman, 'Cricket Master' in *Collected Poems* (1970) p362

94 *Prospectus of Trent Park College of Education* (1965)

95 Ibid, (1973)

96 Ibid

97 *North Circular*, 8 March 1991

98 Ibid, 8 May 1991

99 *Barnet and Finchley Press*, 14 May 1992

100 *Cheshunt and Waltham Telegraph*, 14 May 1992

101 Douglas Dawson, Conservation Committee Chair, oral information

102 William Shakespeare, *A Winter's Tale*, IV, 3, 118-9

103 A dozen or so lots originally collected at Trent Park by Sir Philip Sassoon were auctioned at the sale including a pair of Queen Anne girandoles (mirrors), a stool, and scarlet chest; George II sidetables; George III lacquer bookcases and secretaire, a Flemish tapestry, 18th century English and Portuguese carpets. The sale of *all* items realised over £21m. See *Catalogue* for details and illustrations.

104 *The Diary of John Evelyn* ed ES De Beer (1959) p626

VIII
List of illustrations

Cover	Trent Park (Photograph courtesty of Tony Saunders)
1	Engraving of Trent Park, mid 19th century (Hodson and Ford, *History of Enfield,* 1873)
2	Trent Place, 1808 (Engraving by Sturt, 1808)
3	The Bevan Family at Trent Park, c1888 (N Webster, *Spacious Days*)
4	The staff at Trent Park, c1888 (N Webster, *Spacious Days*)
5	Trent Park north front, 1890 (N Webster, *Spacious Days*)
6	Trent Park south front, 1890 (N Webster, *Spacious Days*)
7	Sir Philip Sassoon by John Singer Sargent, 1923 The Tate Gallery (Photograph courtesy of the Tate Gallery)
8	The south front with its 1890s facade of mauve brick (Photograph courtesy of *Country Life*)
9	The south front, 1931 (Photograph courtesy of *Country Life*)
10	Ground floor plan of Trent Park, 1931 (Courtesy of *Country Life*)
11	Zoffany: The Colmore Family: over the Drawing Room chimney piece, 1931 (Photograph courtesy of *Country Life*)
12	Looking west: The Drawing Room, 1931 (Photograph courtesy of *Country Life*)
13	Looking east: The Drawing Room, 1931 (Photograph courtesy of *Country Life*)
14	Lacquer and Delft ware in the Drawing Room, 1931 (Photograph courtesy of *Country Life*)
15	Enfilade from Library, through Saloon, to Drawing Room, 1931 (Photograph courtesy of *Country Life*)
16	New overmantel panel in the Blue Room: printed in red and blue by Mr Rex Whistler, 1931 (Photograph courtesy of *Country Life*)
17(a)	The Blue Room, pale grey walls, red lacquer, 1931 (Photograph courtesy of *Country Life*) see fig 18 for detail
17(b)	The Blue Room, Trent Park by Winston Churchill. Exhibition Royal Academy, 1948.
18	A Queen Anne scarlet and gilt-japanned bachelor's chest/writing table from the 'Blue Room', 1931 (Photograph courtesy of Christie's)
19(a)	The Library: deep yellow walls, 1931 (Photograph courtesy of *Country Life*) See fig 20 for detail of furniture
19(b)	The Library: Looking West, 1931 (Photograph courtesy of *Country Life*)
20	A pair of George III bow-fronted Chinese aubergine lacquer and satinwood dwarf open bookcases from the library, 1931 (Photograph courtesy of Christie's)
21	The Saloon: buff and quiet green, 1931 (Photograph courtesy of *Country Life*)
22	The Saloon with matching pair of George II side tables, 1931 (Photograph courtesy of *Country Life*) (see fig 23 for detail)
23	One of pair of early George II gilt-gesso side tables, 1931 (Photograph courtesy of Christie's)
24	Dining room (now the Green Room) showing Chinese screen, Zoffany conversation piece of young family and Whistler monogram, 1931 (Photograph courtesy of *Country Life*)

25	A side table in the dining room, 1931 (Photograph courtesy of *Country Life*)
26	The corridor crossing the Entrance Hall. Staircase just in view, 1931 (Photograph courtesy of *Country Life*)
27	The Wistaria Walk (Pergola), 1990 (Photograph Audrey Jemmett)
28	Daffodils in front of the Mansion, 1982 (Photograph Tony Saunders)
29	Lily Ponds, 1931 (Photograph courtesy of *Country Life*)
30	The flower borders, June 1930 (Photograph courtesy of *Country Life*)
31	Swimming pool and orangery, looking east, 1931 (Photograph courtesy of *Country Life*)
32a	The Emma Crewe 'Pineapple' acquired by Sir Philip Sassoon from Wrest Park in 1934 (Photograph Patrick Campbell)
32b	Renaissance statuary brought to Trent Park in the late 1920s (Photograph Patrick Campbell)
32c	Renaissance statuary on the lawn to the left of the mansion terrace (late 1920s) (Photograph Patrick Campbell)
32d	Music block under construction, mansion in background. July 1971
32e	Music block under construction, showing lily pond. July 1971
32f	Library block under construction, refectory block in background. September 1971
33	Trent Park: Cockfosters drive today (Photograph Patrick Campbell)
34(a)	Fireworks Concert: June 1994 (Photograph courtesy of John Rifkin)
34(b)	Prince Edward is greeted by David Peacock for the Royal Gala performance of *Man of La Mancha*, June 1990. (Photograph Tony Saunders)
35	A George III Chinese lacquer burgaute and black and gilt-japanned secretaire cabinet-on-stand in Sir Philip Sassoon's bedroom, 1931 (Photograph courtesy of Christie's)
36	The young family, by Zoffany. The Dining Room, Trent Park, 1931 (Photograph courtesy of *Country Life*)
37	A corner of the Blue Room at Trent Park, 1931 (Photograph courtesy of *Country Life*)
38	One of a pair of Queen Anne scarlet and gilt-japanned girandoles (pier glasses) from the Blue Room, 1931 (Photograph courtesy of *Country Life*)
39	An English needlework carpet with a floral border. 18th Century. From the Saloon., 1931 (Photograph courtesy of *Country Life*)
40	A Portuguese Arraiolos Armorial Carpet with arms of the Dempster of Mures. Early 18th Century. From the Blue Room, 1931 (Photograph courtesy of *Country Life*)
41a	Ludgrove Hall, 1983 (now Middlesex University Conference Centre) (Photograph Frank Jeffs)
41b	Ludgrove Hall (aerial view), 1982 (Photograph courtesy of Aerofilms Ltd)
41c	The Saloon, 1995 (Photograph courtesy of H Morris)
41d	The Drawing Room, 1995 (now the Staff Room) (Photograph courtesy of HJ Morris)
41e	The Stable Block, 1995 (Photograph Patrick Campbell)
41f	Trent Country Park, 1995 (Photograph Patrick Campbell)
41g	A university relaxes, 1995 (Photograph Patrick Campbell)
41h	Terrace in winter looking west (Photograph Audrey Jemmett)
41i	The Principal's Lodge, formerly Dowerhouse of Hannah Gubbay, 1997 (Photograph Tony Saunders)
41j	Aerial view of Trent Country Park showing the Middlesex University campus, 1992 (Photograph

[Fig 18] A Queen Anne scarlet and gilt-japanned bachelor's chest/writing table from the 'Blue Room'. 1931

[Fig 20] A pair of George III bow-fronted Chinese aubergine lacquer and satinwood dwarf open bookcases from the library. 1931

[Fig 23] One of a pair of early George II gilt-gesso side tables. 1931

[Fig 35] A George III Chinese lacquer burgaute and black and gilt-japanned secretaire cabinet-on-stand in Sir Philip Sassoon's bedroom. 1931

[Fig 39] An English needlework carpet with a floral border. 18th Century. From the Saloon. 1931

[Fig 38] One of a pair of Queen Anne scarlet and gilt-japanned girandoles (pier glasses) from the Blue Room. 1931

[Fig 40] A Portuguese Arraiolos Armorial Carpet with arms of the Dempster of Mures. Early 18th Century. From the Blue Room. 1931

[Fig 41c]
The Saloon, 1995

[Fig 41d]
The Drawing Room, 1995 (now the Staff Room)

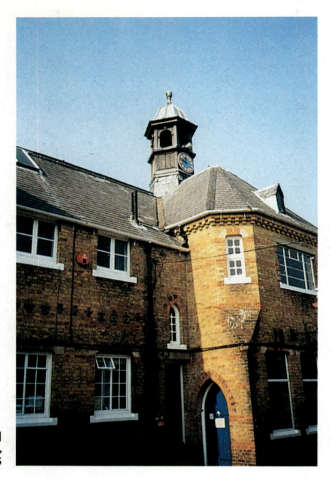

[Fig 41e]
The Stable Block,
1995

[Fig 41f]
Trent Country
Park, 1995

[Fig 41g]
A university relaxes, 1995

[Fig 34a]
Fireworks Concert
June 1994

[Fig 41h]
Terrace in winter looking west

[Fig 41i] The Principal's Lodge, formerly Dowerhouse of Hannah Gubbay

[Fig 41j] Aerial view of Trent Country Park showing the Middlesex University campus, 1992